Find Your

UNIQUE VALUE Proposition

In Principle & Practice

To Dominate Your Real Estate Market

Rowena Patton

Edited by M.L. Hunt

For my beloved Grandad, Ronald Patton, who threw me into 'the deep end' at a young age, knowing I would swim.

Foreword by Dave Ulrich

"The Value of Values" - Introduction by
Dave Ulrich

"I'VE KNOWN ROWENA
PATTON SINCE 1996, AND I'M
SO PLEASED THAT SHE IS
BRINGING THE UNIQUE VALUE
PROPOSITION CONCEPT TO
THE REAL ESTATE INDUSTRY"

DAVE ULRICH

In the last 20 years, almost every organization - public or private, large or small, domestic or global - has discussed both values, and value. 'Values' often represent core beliefs, and shape the daily behavior of leaders. 'Value' is how those values are used to help someone else.

Value focuses outside; values come from within. Value emphasizes what others get from our efforts; values emphasize who we are. Value can be created and developed through innovation and hard work; values are generally inherited, and may be honed through self-awareness and experience. Value can be measured by impact; values are measured by the strength of our character. Value derives from the worth of our work to stakeholders; values reflect the worth of our work to us.

If the receiver defines value, it is helpful to know if an organization's values resonate with top customers. It is helpful to ask these customers if your organization's values matter to them. Generally, with values like innovation, collaboration, service, respect, the answer is 'yes.' But, in one case, the organization's primary value was 'to be the most profitable in the industry' - and the customer quickly said this was not what mattered most to the customer. Customer value begins with *them being part of defining desired values.*

Value statements make core beliefs more explicit. But when values become the basis of customer discussions and commitments, the value of values increases dramatically. This is an example of 'outside in' work that defines effective organizations not just by what is done, but how it adds value to key stakeholders.

Dave Ulrich has published over 200 articles and book chapters and over 25 books. He edited Human Resource Management 1990-1999, served on editorial boards of 4 Journals, on the Board of Directors for Herman Miller, and Board of Trustees at Southern Virginia University, and is a Fellow in the National Academy of Human Resources.

Dave Ulrich Rensis Likert Professor of Business, University of Michigan, Partner, the RBL Group www.daveulrich.com

Contents

Introduction

This book was written by top real estate agent Rowena Patton, Keller Williams International's '2007 #3 Rookie of the Year', a 60m producer and developer of team-building systems and customer programs used by the AllStar Network of agents around the country. It was written for real estate agents wanting to convert more home browsers to home buyers, and more home value-checkers to home sellers. It's for those agents wanting to convert more prospects into clients, and more clients into forever clients, who provide repeat and referral business throughout an agent's career.

One proven way to accomplish this is being able to offer something of *value* that is different - something which sets them apart from the rest of the real estate crowd. Indeed, everyone in real estate, or any business for that matter, needs a Unique Value Proposition (UVP). A well-rounded Unique Value Proposition will *identify* target customers, *define what's being offered* and how that offer *solves a problem*, as well as how it is *different from any existing alternatives*.

An agent's Unique Value Proposition is often derived from their passion - that which has driven them to take action throughout the course of their lives. Often one's UVP is already present, though perhaps buried under multiple layers, and 'the noise of life.' While we all have a passion for something, it's surprising to find how re-examining, identifying and harnessing that energy can provide a stronger foundation in your real estate business. Constructing a new foundation with building blocks which already exist makes it much easier, even fun, to accomplish.

It's a fast-paced industry. Agents hoping to get ahead in this crowded marketplace need something which distinguishes them from their competitors, and makes them the 'agent of choice' on that first phone call or meeting. The vast majority of the time, a buyer or seller will begin their real estate journey online. Once there, the unsuspecting buyer or seller clicks a button - usually titled something like: *Find Out More* - enters their phone number, and *Boom!* They've become an 'Internet lead,' with at least three agents relentlessly calling, texting and emailing them to win their business... and the race begins.

Still, the average *conversion* of these Internet leads is about 2% - meaning that a lot of time, energy and finances will be invested, for a relatively small return. 'Speed to lead' is paramount in increasing a conversion rate, yet it's still something that many busy agents, often out with clients, find difficult to accomplish. Defining your own Unique Value Proposition and using Programs which are UVPs will drastically improve upon that conversion rate.

Sellers often begin their home sale by interviewing two or three listing agents, who are counting mostly upon their training, personality and 'years in the business' to get them across the finish line. However, without a clear Unique Value Proposition in place, those assets may not be the agents' strongest competitive advantage - as other agents will likely share those same attributes.

"A CLEAR UVP WILL SET THE FOUNDATION FOR BUILDING A SALABLE BUSINESS, ONE WHICH HAS VALUE FAR BEYOND THE FOUNDER'S DIRECT INVOLVEMENT"

A clear UVP will set the foundation for building a salable business, one which has value far beyond both the founder's direct involvement, or marquee value. Over time, any strong enterprise should have developed both its Unique Value Proposition, as well as its business.

This book also raises questions about what have become core foundations in today's real estate, while addressing three main concepts behind the **Unique Value Proposition**:

1. Determining **your Natural Affinity Audience,** by better defining and communicating what is unique about you.

2. Creating **Marketing Strategies and Systems** designed to shift 'transactional relationships' into long-term client relationships.

3. Providing you with **Programs**, which will remove obstacles to success, long before they happen.

Defining your own UVP requires some self-investigation and patience. The good news is, everyone's UVP already exists somewhere within their life and business experiences, yet defining a reliable one almost always requires more delving. This may sound easy, however, while teaching classes on this subject, I've met scores of agents who continue to experience the same frustrating obstacles, without any clear understanding *as to why.* These obstacles take many forms, and are often symptoms of poorly defined UVPs, or programs. Here is an example of a typical conversation that I have with agents:

"I thought my **specialty** *was selling real estate.* I feel overwhelmed by systems I've collected, or used over the years, all the leads I felt I had to purchase; they've all added up to a big pile of 'shiny objects,' which aren't always helping that much.

"THERE'S ALL THE ROLES I PLAY, THE EXTRA COURSES, ENDLESS PRESSURE TO GET CONTRACTS, TO MAKE ENDS MEET. I FEEL LIKE I'M ON A HAMSTER WHEEL."

Then there's all the roles I play, the extra courses, endless pressure to get contracts, to make ends meet. I feel like I'm on a **hamster wheel.**"

Again, in teaching my classes, I've heard multiple versions of this from both new and experienced agents. We've all been on that 'hamster wheel' at one point or another!

To identify the source of these frustrations, I reviewed my own real estate processes, business relationships and experiences, and recognized that two keys to unlocking this mystery lie in: 1). Agents more clearly defining their own Unique Value Proposition, and 2). Better communicating Value to their clients. Both of these subject areas are covered in detail in this book. I've also shared the wisdom, mentorship and guidance of those I was fortunate enough to find as I made my real estate journey, whose direction began a continual state of learning. One of those mentors was Orlando-based, Keller Williams / MAPS Coach Mike Krantz, who became a coach and key person in my life.

Mike Krantz's take on *Unique Value Proposition*:

"It's important for every real estate agent to have a clear and precise value proposition, so that potential customers can clearly see what value the agent is bringing to the table. When we do not have clarity on our value, then how is the consumer to have clarity on what we feel is important about our business? What it actually gets down to is us having to stand apart from our competition, as well as creating a central focal point for a team - all working together to achieve a standard of value."

Mike Kranz, MAPS Coach and Rainmaker

Your Unique Value Proposition should be the backbone of your business.

Do you have your Unique Value Proposition figured out? If not, I suggest you make discovering your UVP a main priority before continuing to build your transactional business. Once you do, your UVP will shine out in front of you and your business, and become your magnet, permeating everything you do. It will do most of your heavy lifting for you.

My Big 'Why'

Real estate can take its toll on anyone, and despite my early successes, I was no exception! Somewhere along the way - while understanding that most aspects of a rewarding life were based on successful relation-

"YOUR UVP WILL SHINE OUT IN FRONT OF YOU AND YOUR BUSINESS, AND BECOME YOUR MAGNET, PERMEATING EVERYTHING YOU DO"

ships - I began to realize that *yesterday's real estate* process is loaded with the very obstacles that *derail good relationships*. From the beginning, maintaining great business relationships in real estate became akin to keeping a life raft afloat in high winds, over shark-infested waters!

Buyers wondered what, if anything, was really wrong with the house? Could they really afford this? Would their old furniture really fit in the new home?

Sellers had their own share of concerns; they were often parting with their home, the place where their family was raised. They needed to figure out how to choose an agent who would really help them deal with things like deferred maintenance, the reorganization and cleanup to place their home on the market, etc. As an agent, I wondered: was I really addressing these concerns in a systematic way?

Eventually, the stack of concerns and objections from both buyers and sellers grew so high, they had eclipsed whatever joy I was hoping to get out of the business, and clouded the success I experienced early on as one of the top three agents in my first year at Keller Williams International.

"THE STACK OF CONCERNS AND OBJECTIONS FROM BOTH BUYERS AND SELLERS GREW SO HIGH, THEY HAD ECLIPSED WHATEVER JOY I WAS HOPING TO GET OUT OF THE BUSINESS"

Meanwhile, the industry had also gained some shadowy DNA in the 'reputation department.' Consider that in 2006, Harris Interactive published a poll listing 'the most trusted professions.' While doctors topped the list - with fifty percent of respondents putting docs in the "completely trusted" category - real estate agents neared the bottom, barely beating out stockbrokers, lagging auto mechanics, lawyers and insurance agents! Who wanted to be *in that category?* Not me.

Though I was experiencing commercial success, something clearly wasn't right. Even rudimentary steps were taking too much time. Trust between parties often seemed poorly established, too fragile or too easily broken. As exciting as buying or selling a home should have been, this was *often not the case.* Too often, what both agents and customers experienced was anxiety, dread, and confusion. Where does all this pain, stress and frustration come from?

The excitement was always palpable when an offer was placed on a home, and later when an agent would get the call saying, "Congratulations, the offer was accepted." Then, when that offer became a contract, the real work began - often resembling an emotional and logistical roller coaster - throughout the inspection, appraisal and re-negotiation process. Still - after all this - contracts failed *almost one-third of the time.* Why?

The anxiety people feel throughout the old real estate process remains real, and does not change. What *can* change *is the process,* and how we approach the inherent challenges along the way. This convinced me to begin creating a new approach, from a new perspective.

The first section of the book focuses on finding *your own Unique Value Proposition,* which helps you develop stronger and clearer channels of communication based on trust. The second section introduces *UVP Programs* which will help you further develop that trust, using better real estate processes which will reinforce good business relationships. They will help you identify the obstacles, gain understanding and control of the more damaging ones and clear them up *before* they wreak havoc, and cause undue stress. The third section delves into where some of my perspectives were developed.

I'll explain how the UVP Programs came about, and why they work. The Programs featured in the book are being used by the AllStarCertified agents at their headquarters, AllStarPowerhouse in Asheville NC, and a number of agents in other locations in our AllStarCertified Network; all have passed the tests of time, in terms of efficiency and results.

Perhaps the biggest objective of this book is to help you find **your** Unique Value Proposition, and *put those ideas into action*. There is also a companion workbook to this book, along with coaching and classes, which you can learn more details about at www.UVPBook.com to help you *get into action faster*.

> "SHINE A LIGHT ON THE PATH,
> SUCH THAT OTHERS
> FIND THEIR MAGIC.
> WE'VE ALL GOT IT, SOMETIMES
> IT'S JUST HARD TO SEE."
>
> ROWENA PATTON

Finally - your success stories feed my soul. I've been hearing them in small group settings for years; stories of listings won using the Programs featured in this book, or UVP concepts and techniques that were put into action. Watching people grow drives me; the big 'why' in my life is to 'Shine a light on the path, such that others find their magic.' And yes - *everyone* has magic!

How The Book Is Organized

Chapter 1: Finding Your Unique Value Proposition, helps you better understand the UVP concept by exploring and identifying what is unique about you - what you love to do, and what you are passionate about - and tying that into your real estate business. This is accomplished through a common theme in business relationships: developing a stronger sense of trust and deeper connections with your clients, *based on shared values, backgrounds, and interests*.

Chapter 2: AllStarCertified's UVP Programs address *the process* first, as a foundation for how you conduct your business. All Programs are fueled largely by 'anticipatory intelligence' - what we can do to help buyers and sellers enjoy the process more, and experience a better result - by anticipating stress points before they arrive, and derail your business relationship. Each Program addresses a customer issue I've experienced along the way.

Chapter 3: About the Author - Where the Perspective Came From, shares more details about my life and work experiences, and insight into where many of my perspectives stemmed from.

You will find icons throughout the book, to assist with searching more quickly for scripts, links, footnotes, key points and the like.

For further exploration, a companion workbook is available, as well as classes which will help you further develop and implement the ideas that interest you. For more details, please visit www.UVPBook.com

Workbook

Chapter 1:

Finding Your Unique Value Proposition

U nique Value Propositions are those specific qualities you exhibit, and the different ways you go about interacting with your clients that clearly set you apart from your competition. While some agents initially have a hard time understanding it, everyone holds the key to at least one or more Unique Value Propositions.

The UVP concept permeates everything I teach around the country. To best grasp the full weight and strength of the UVP concept, my classes incorporate both a tested *process of elimination* mixed with some *honest self-examination*. In my classes, this often begins with one seemingly simple question:

"If you had to guess,
what would you say your Unique Value Proposition is?"

Agents' answers are written on a white-board, and include ideas such as 'placing listings on 400 websites,' and 'possessing better negotiation skills.' These are what I call *'Givens'* (which we'll explore shortly) - and while these are important skills to master, they are not UVPs. After this point, there are often concerned looks around the room as we review, and strike through the white-board list, one by one. Occasionally, we may discover one UVP from the room, out of the 30 or more ideas offered up.

- PLACE THE LISTING ON THE MLS WITHIN 24 HOURS
- PRICE IT PROPERLY
- GREAT LOOKING SIGN IN THE YARD
- SECURE LOCKBOX ON THE DOOR
- TAKE GOOD PHOTOS
- ADVERTISE IN A REAL ESTATE MAGAZINE
- ADVERTISE THE LISTING ON 400+ WEBSITES
- NEGOTIATE BETTER
- COMMUNICATE MORE OFTEN
- MAKE RECOMMENDATIONS FOR STAGING THE HOME

At this stage, we take a moment to consider a real estate scenario:

Imagine you're at a listing appointment, standing in line with two other agents from your brokerage. The sellers are giving each agent 10 minutes to present, as they want to know:

"Why you?"

Scenario

When you go inside the home, what key points are you underscoring in order to set yourself apart? Is what you are presenting a 'Given' or a true *UVP*? Compare your answers to the 'white-board' list. Do you see anything in common?

There's an important difference between providing services which customers *already expect*, known hereafter as 'Givens,' versus a service which can and will *set you apart from your competition*, known hereafter as a 'Unique Value Proposition', or UVP.

Let's Define A Term: 'Givens'

Definition

'Givens' are **services your clients will expect any professional real estate agent to offer.** Therefore, they are *not your Unique Value Proposition.* Still, agents often confuse them with UVPs.

> "GIVENS ARE STEPS YOUR CLIENTS WILL EXPECT ANY PROFESSIONAL REAL ESTATE AGENT TO TAKE, THEY ARE NOT YOUR UNIQUE VALUE PROPOSITION"
>
> ROWENA PATTON

Let's revisit the question: "If you had to guess, what would you say *your Unique Value Proposition is?*"

Agents' answers often outline traditional real estate basics, such as great customer service and the quality of their offerings.

These are known as *'Givens.'* They are important aspects of how we do our business - however, it's also *expected* that we offer these services. Most agents will offer them. They are not a *point of differentiation,* or Unique Value Proposition, as customers will always expect 'going rates,' 'reasonable levels of service,' 'traditional activities' and professionalism.

While they may not all be truly unique, UVPs will provide you with a better chance to overtake your competition – especially if they are something that 80% of your competition *are not able* or *willing to do.* Of course, if 100% of your competitors aren't doing it, even better.

Executive Assistant to top agent and MAPS Coach, Kathy Oakes, Catherine Spitznagel said it best:

"It's hard to fail at something *when you're the only one doing it!"*

During a memorable teaching event, one of the students offered up what they thought might be their unique value proposition:

"I get back to people within 24 hours."

The room went silent.

Some people say things like, "I do better marketing." That isn't well defined. It's an empty statement, which will not get most people excited. Always ask yourself, what do I mean by that, specifically, then chop it down to bite-sized pieces, which should include measurable numbers and examples of what you actually do.

"I GET BACK TO PEOPLE WITHIN 24 HOURS"

ANONYMOUS

To get a better idea of where I'm going with this, let's take a quick look at Rosser Reeves. Reeves is widely appreciated as the person who introduced the Unique *Sales* Proposition concept, which has emerged, over the years, as the Unique Value Proposition concept - and wrote a popular book called **Reality In Advertising.**

In that book, Reeves outlined his concept:

1. Every advertisement must make a proposition to the consumer - not just words, or product 'puffery'. Tell the audience why they should buy and what specific benefit they will derive.

2. Advertise a benefit that your competition doesn't offer, such as a uniqueness of brand or a new claim.

Reeves states: "Your unique selling proposition must be so strong that it will compel customers to shift to your product."

The Unique Value Proposition Test: The '80% Rule' & The 'So What' Rule

There are Two Rules to apply to *anything* you may consider to be your Unique Value Proposition. Note: it's a great idea to brainstorm at this point - to come up with a few ideas, which you think are strong. The two rules that make up the UVP Test are:

1. One is the '**80%' Rule**: are 80% or more agents already doing the thing that you came up with?

2. The second is the '**So What' Rule**: is your idea of any real interest to your customers?

Once you have an idea of what your Unique Value Proposition is, pass it through the **UVP Test**: two key questions which help you define the validity of whether your offering is a Unique Value Proposition, *or a 'Given'* - and whether people care enough about it to become a strong enough foundation for your business.

The UVP Test™

Rowena Patton's UVP Test

Question 1: Are most of your competitors not offering your UVP: does it pass the '**80% Rule**'?

Question 2: Do customers even care about your idea: does it pass the '**So What**' rule?

UVP passes the '80% and So What rules' Congratulations - start work on threading your UVP throughout your business

1. The 80% Rule

Do 80% of competitors (or more) claim that they offer a similar service, Program or product that is your proposed UVP? If the answer is "Yes," then it's not a UVP.

UVPs need to be exciting to your customer, and something that almost no one, or at least most others, are not offering. If you're thinking 'if even *one other person* offers that value' that it's not unique - you are technically correct. However, you can offer it with a *'twist'* - offer even more value and make it your own. For example, an 'Open House' held in a traditional fashion is a 'Given.' When you offer an Open House Program *in a manner which clearly sets you apart,* that may be enough of a 'twist' to make it a Unique Value Proposition.

Now that you have an understanding of the '80% Rule,' apply it to the previous list of agent's ideas for their UVPs from the 'Givens' section. The '80% Rule' will eliminate many of your early ideas. Let's revisit that white-board list, shown here.

- PLACE THE LISTING ON THE MLS WITHIN 24 HOURS

- PRICE IT PROPERLY

- GREAT LOOKING SIGN IN THE YARD

- SECURE LOCKBOX ON THE DOOR

- TAKE GOOD PHOTOS

  GIVENS

- ADVERTISE IN A REAL ESTATE MAGAZINE

- ADVERTISE THE LISTING ON 400+ WEBSITES

- NEGOTIATE BETTER

- COMMUNICATE MORE OFTEN

- MAKE RECOMMENDATIONS FOR STAGING THE HOME

2: The 'So What' Rule

When your idea **has** passed the '**80% Rule**,' does your proposed UVP pass the '**So What' Rule**? Ask these questions: does it really pique their **interest**? Do your customers **really care** about this offer - and if so, how much? What great benefit does your offer provide for them? What problems are you solving for them, which others are not? Have you tested the idea out with your audience? Have you run it by a few people whom you trust to give you candid feedback?

Learn More

If you'd like to study more on this, I highly recommend undertaking Keller Williams '*6 Personal Perspectives*' training program. Visit Step 3. '*From Entrepreneurial to Purposeful*,' in order to better understand the steps to break through your '*Fundamental ceiling of achievement*.' One of those steps will be to seek out mentors, who may be running with some-thing similar already.

Upon confirming that your UVP resolves your customers' issues, you will have a UVP that you can build upon. However, even applying both of these rules only gets you to the planning stage for your UVP!

NOTE: TAKE HEART! DON'T WORRY ABOUT THE 'GRAVEYARD OF IDEAS' YOU'LL INITIALLY COME UP WITH, BECAUSE WE'VE ALL BEEN THERE. THOSE IDEAS MAY STILL EXIST HAPPILY AS 'GIVENS,' WHICH WILL BEEF UP YOUR 'LISTING PRESENTATION' AND OTHER MARKETING MATERIALS, WHICH WE'LL EXPLORE IN GREATER DETAIL LATER IN THE BOOK!

Leverage Your UVP

When defining our UVPs, it's critical to be specific about what your unique points are, and even more importantly, *what benefit they offer to your customer.*

Scenario

For example, I would go to a **listing appointment (or have a phone conversation)** and say:

Script

Me: *"I know your listing expired and I'm sorry for the frustration and wasted time that must've caused you. Was your house listed with a **Listing Storyboard**?"*

Seller: *"A what?"*

Me: *"Our **Listing Storyboard** comprises a Walking-Tour Video and an interview with the sellers, followed up by comments from family and friends who know interesting details about the property."*

More to the point, I can now immediately *set myself apart from other agents* by explaining how it works, and why it's important.

Me: *"Have you seen anything like that before?"*

Seller: *"No!"*

Currently, AllStarCertified agents are the only ones who use the AllStar **Listing Storyboard™** (one of over 12 UVP's AllStarCertified agents use). You'll learn more about the customer need this Program addresses later in this book. Remember, as an agent, you don't need a dozen UVPs, you really only need one - a great one - that you're passionate about.

Learn More

For more information, I suggest reading Gary Keller and Jay Papasan's book *"The ONE Thing"* about why focusing on one thing is so important. Note: most effective UVPs can replace 'Listing Storyboard' in the above script.

The best UVPs come from addressing a customer need and creating something others haven't thought of, or done yet. For example, the **Listing Storyboard** grew from my frustrations in only having an 'MLS sheet' or website property link to share with potential buyers. I wanted to send buyers something that told a richer and more complete story of the home. To address that need, I created something that *provided more value.*

As a real estate agent, your Unique Value Proposition becomes your foundation - whenever networking, out in public, face-to-face, while using social media and other methods of communicating your message - it is front and center.

Script

For example, take what I call 'The Grocery Story Speech' (often referred to as 'the elevator speech').

It goes something like this: you walk into a grocery store, carrying a tote bag, or wearing a name badge which identifies you as an agent.

As you lean in to grab some avocados, someone asks you: *"So, how's the real estate market?"*

How would you respond, in a compelling way, in just a few short minutes?

What does one say next? (HINT): What is *different* about you?

Perhaps they'll follow with, *"You know, I'm thinking about selling my house."*

Consider these two different replies:

1. *"That's great! My company offers a **Certified Pre-Owned** Program - have you ever heard of that approach?"* - Immediately going into that differentiation.

2. Or simply: *"The real estate market is great. It's a good time to sell."*

Take a moment to consider which is more effective in 1) differentiating yourself from other agents, while opening up a conversation, and 2) a statement which essentially closes the conversation, or waits for them to drive the next sentence.

Are you still scratching your head because the concept of your Unique Value Proposition is hazy, rather than concrete? Let's delve in more.

A Framework For Creating YOUR Unique Value Proposition

Now that we've defined some terms and concepts, let's discover *your* Unique Value Proposition. We'll explore the experience, knowledge, and passion that are uniquely yours, and apply them to real estate, in order to attract your **Natural Affinity Audience.** Once we've defined that audience, we'll look at what **Marketing Strategies and Systems** you can use to best reach that audience.

When you've researched your customer needs, there will likely be **Programs** that you can develop to address those needs. The following sections outline how to both identify and communicate things you already know, only in a broader fashion. Remember: your knowledge and experience *truly set you apart*; they can and should form the *framework for your specialty.*

UVP - The Three Building Blocks: Affinity Audience, Marketing Content And Programs

Building Block 1. Affinity Audience.
Determining what is unique about you, in order to attract your Natural Affinity Audience.

Definition

A Natural Affinity Audience is a group of people you have something in common with, through something you share - such as language, work experience, interests or culture. Truly understanding your Natural Affinity Audience can become the basis for your Unique Value Proposition.

While prospecting, have you ever noticed how easily the conversation flows once you've determined you have something in common with the prospective client? While this may seem obvious at first glance, I cannot tell you how many classes I've taught where people are not examining who their Natural Affinity Audiences *really are*.

To define your Natural Affinity Audience, start off with these questions:

1. Geography - where have I lived, what's my heritage?

2. Work Experience and connections - what does my resume look like?

3. What's my Cultural Heritage?

4. What languages do I speak?

5. What Hobbies and Interests do I have?

6. What is my family structure?

7. What do I specialize in?

1. Geography

One example most agents relate to is a Natural Affinity Audience based on *geography*.

Example   You're on the phone with a prospective buyer or seller, and learn that you've both lived in the same town, city, or part of the world. It could also be a school you both went to, a common language you speak, or a career you share (or shared). Suddenly, a firm bond is established; why wouldn't *you* become their agent of choice? You have a natural affinity with these folks, yet may not be finding a way to attract and ***own that audience.***

2. Your Previous Work Experience And Connections

Example

Remember that your previous career need not be 'checked at the door' when you enter real estate! Your **previous work experience** is another powerful way to differentiate yourself. For example:

You were a nurse in your previous career. How might that help you in real estate? You have a natural affinity for helping people, and the 'likability' factor (hopefully!) and 'people skills' you've learned in nursing are *absolutely* applicable to real estate. Along these lines, make *a new list* of the skills, which can benefit you in your real estate business.

You were a teacher. Put on your real estate garb and call around the schools; explain that you're working with a lot of buyers from out of the area, and that they're always asking you about schools. Make an appointment to go and see the principal, or school manager and learn *their UVP*. Publish whatever they allow you to, such as an interview with the principal. Once you've interviewed five or six key principals in that area, imagine what you will have learned - and can now share. Note: This can work in many previous work scenarios where the industry serves the public.

Whether the field involved Dentists, Doctors, Nurseries, Hospitals or Schools - you have a natural 'in,' as you 'used to be a Teacher, understand the business, *and speak their language*.' This is best handled on a *blog*, so you can leverage it later - posting it out on social media and other channels - and allowing more people to comment on what you've written (more about that later). Imagine the rich results you could create!

You worked in a dentist's office. Something as simple as wearing your real estate garb, going into a dental office and introducing yourself, along with your stack of business cards, could easily bring you more business. If you worked in a business-to-consumer (or B2C) business, make a list of the 20+ offices within a 20-minute drive, and go visit them!

You could introduce yourself with something like: "I used to work in a dentist's office and yours is impressive. I work with a lot of buyers in the

Script

area, and would love to add you to the list of offices I provide; would that be okay?" Start developing a list of all of those offices, share them with clients - and don't forget to keep visiting. A similar strategy works with any 'affinity groups,' so think about how to monetize whatever your 'group' may be.

These concepts work whenever and wherever you had contact with the public, whether you've worked with Police, as a Firefighter, Veteran or Military office. Get the idea?

Here's an example of leveraging your previous work experience and connections.

Orlando, Fl. agent Jessica Estrada worked in hospitality for many years, and we discussed how she could leverage that experience. Jessica works with potential buyers who are not currently living in the Orlando area, and knows that providing some insight as to where they can stay when they visit will be *valuable to them.*

In order to gain a better sense of their overall operations, Jessica meets with the management of several top-rated hotels in her area. These are easy meetings for her, as she speaks the 'hospitality language.' The end result is two-fold: first, Jessica has content to share with her buyers, providing an overview of multiple hotels as 'a short read.' Second: she also meets many 'multipliers' - people who will meet many others - who are likely to have questions about real estate. By leveraging her work experience, Jessica has fun back in her old domain while placing herself as 'the go-to agent' for that audience. This puts her prospecting on steroids!

3. Cultural Heritage

Example

It could be your **cultural heritage**. While many agents may steer away from this, it's worth examining; if you come from another country, chances are there are some people in your 'neck of the woods' that came from the same place. Why not put a Program together that markets to that portion of the population? It may be a small population, however there's no reason you couldn't easily 'own' that audience.

You are of **Greek heritage**. You can communicate about Greek restaurants, Greek churches and anything else connected to your heritage. You can become conversant about Greek aspects inherent to your location, and soon even become somewhat of an expert on Greek culture in your city. When you become the 'go-to' person for your culture, explore how to monetize that relationship - or make sure you're getting referrals for clients. *'Own' that sector!*

Note: this can apply to any culture. Culture can also be applied to a group with which you have a natural affinity (read: LGBTQ, African American, etc.)

4. Foreign Language

"WHATEVER YOU DO, GIVE ME SOMEONE WHO DOESN'T SPEAK CHINESE"

You speak a **foreign language**. Now more than ever, the US has become an even bigger melting pot - and there are obviously many different languages which people have connections to. Chances are good there are others who speak the same language as you in your city - even if it's a relatively small group. Why not decide to be the 'go-to' real estate agent for that small group of people? That group may well turn out to be larger than you suspected, and often does.

To this suggestion, the most common objection many agents give is: "No one *else* would want to work with me." -It doesn't work that way. It reflects having a mindset of abundance, not scarcity. Flexibility, not rigidness. If someone's searching online for a Spanish speaker or a Chinese speaker, you will 'pop up.' They *won't* search using the terms: "whatever you do, give me someone who doesn't speak Chinese!"

Typical Objection

Example

You speak *French* **(insert any language other than English - though even English can be divided into 'Southern,' or other dialects).** Do you have a blog written in French? A Facebook page that's in French? Celebrate the French culture in your area (see Cultural Heritage). Maybe only 2% of your community speaks French; still - what a way to own that territory. You speak 'Southern' - Imagine the fun that you could have with a blog explaining the southern culture - *from your perspective!*

5. Your Interests And hobbies

It's likely that you share an interest with a large portion of the buyers and sellers who are your 'prospects.' Start building content about your key interest and get it out there, so *people can find you* and relate! This is one of the easiest routes to an 'affinity audience,' because you're taking pictures, making videos and writing about something you already love doing.

Example

You used to work in, or have a **love for music**. Assuming you still love what you used to do, develop lists of music shops, music venues, music Programs which schools offer, and music teachers - and visit them. Share your knowledge and passion! Remember that *you already have a huge insight into their life.*

During a teaching event which covered these ideas, a couple that had recently begun their real estate career visited with me during a break. They described, quite emotionally, how they had previously spent decades together as composer and conductor, and were now struggling 'to find a foothold in real estate.' Though once convinced they had to leave their previous 'passions' behind, they came to realize that *they could incorporate their past into their current profession.*

Let's say you like **mountain bike riding**. Do you think any buyers or sellers in your market like mountain-bike riding? Why not feature photos and maps of mountain-bike trails on your website, or your blog? Find out where the concentration of mountain bike trails are located - which you're already somewhat familiar with - because (remember) you love mountain biking. *You are going where your passion is.* Then, pull a radius of houses within 15 - 30 minutes of mountain bike trails, and feature a link to those houses on the blog, or platform you are using. Have photos and videos from your mountain biking expeditions. This won't cost you much time, because again - *you're already passionate about it.*

Perhaps you **love to garden**. What kinds of plants grow where you live? What doesn't do so well? Experiment with different channels to get your message out; 'Facebook live' a video of the shoots pushing through, in spring, and then follow it up showing progress. These concepts can also be applied to issues, or a passion for something - such as being the parent(s) of special-needs children, or expertise on non-GMO foods or the even the environment. Note: some issues may be considered 'hot buttons,' so, *proceed with caution.*

One of Boise Idaho's top agents, Graham MacKenzie, incorporates his real estate business into his love for, and expertise in, being a fly-fishing guide.

"My goal is to become the go-to agent in Boise, Idaho for fly-fishers and trail-runners, when they're thinking 'real estate.' I share my expertise as a licensed fly-fishing guide and passionate trail-runner on blogs and other platforms, and love the discussions that flow from the topics. Whether it's fishing reports, trail reports, upcoming local races, and interviews with local shop owners, gear reviews and maps - there's literally something for everyone.

Whenever possible, I create a link to homes available in those related areas. In addition, I often organize group runs and casting lessons as another avenue for creating value to those participating in these sports. I'm also considering a 1% of gross sales 'giveback' to groups - likely environmental - who support and protect those hobbies. Eventually, I'll look into expansion in areas which are meccas for these activities, and help others do the same."

6. Familial Status

There's always a student in my class that says, "I've *only* **been a parent**, or *single person living with my parents*." -Phooey!

Example

You know about kindergartens, schools, great shops for kid's items, mom's groups, etc. If your parents are older, and you live with them, then you have a huge 'Affinity Audience' right there. You could write about your parents' generation - their values, the Do's and Don'ts to keep one's elderly parents happy, etc. You might examine and find ways to build a budget, in order to afford your own home. What if you provide care for someone in your family? Think of the care facilities you've developed a huge wealth of knowledge about. Get the idea?

7. Real Estate Specialization

Most agents do not specialize in a particular *type of home*. I know this, because I've taught thousands of agents and when I ask what they specialize in, they say: "selling houses." There are a couple ways you can establish what you specialize in. What do you LOVE to sell? Is it:

Historic homes? Condos and town-homes? Golf Course homes? Waterfront, or Oceanfront homes? Farms? Commercial? Starter homes? The list goes on...

Again, the main objection I hear from agents is: "People will not come to me for everything else." -Yet, here's the truth: potential clients are not 'Googling' the term: "real estate agent that *doesn't do* oceanfront homes!"

Typical Objection

Believe it or not, you **do specialize** in something. Whether it's the neighborhood you live in, or any other of the above examples - the content lands in your lap every day, as you drive home or go about your regular activities. Most likely, you are already capturing a quick picture of that sunset on the marina, or a video of something on your way home. Perhaps the history of the area provides a springboard for something, from a quick post to an in in-depth article.

Once you tag a picture of the playground you took on the way home, soon you'll have a number of posts tagged #ThingsForKidsToDoInXYZ (which people can click on, and check out) full of info on kids in your town. That's the 'pull effect' of your marketing. The 'push' effect is when you click on the tag, and post "things to do in my town, with kids." Ultimately, *people care more about lifestyle than bricks and mortar.*

While these examples and questions may seem obvious, upon closer examination you'll find that they hold many keys regarding your Unique Value Proposition. Defining your UVP lies within your life experiences and the lessons you've learned from them; these will always provide a road map towards unlocking the secret to *your true audience*, and how to best communicate with them.

Once your Natural Affinity Audience is defined, you can figure out what you are communicating, and the best platforms for your message. Note: for busy real estate agents, in order to eliminate a 'learning curve,' the best platform to begin with (i.e., social media, print, radio, etc.) is the **one *you're* already using**. You can add more over time, as you master *developing* your content and delivering it more consistently. We will delve into this in the next chapter.

If you're faithful to both finding and reaching out to your Natural Affinity Audience, business *will come* from getting face-to-face time with these folks! Most of them will likely be multipliers; in other words, they might well share your name with many other friends. Consider using the examples above as ways to tie your Natural Affinity Audience *back to real estate!*

Example

Think about it along these lines: imagine a potential client whose interests and experience include a love for tennis - and *you used to be tennis pro*. Don't you think that client would rather work with you on the sale or purchase of a home? Of course they would; you both love the same thing, and you already *speak that language*. Yet, they'll never know you both share those passions until you reveal those things about yourself.

Building Block 2: Creating Marketing Strategies and Systems designed to shift a 'transactional relationship' viewpoint into long-term client relationships.

Marketing Beyond 'One On One.'

Getting answers out of your head, and onto paper.

While many agents may already hold answers to the above questions, I've noticed that quite often, agents tend to store, but not share the valuable information they've collected. It seems that too often, valuable information simply remains between their ears - which I've always considered to be a shame. Why would anyone do this?

Perhaps they feel they should hold onto the 'power' which that information provides, only sharing it when sitting down for a 'face-to-face' meeting, or on a 'one-on-one' basis - such as in a client consultation, or on the phone. Still, when agents accrue valuable information that comprises both their life and real estate experiences - yet allow it to simply remain stored in their head - they're often limiting the use of key elements to their Unique Value Proposition.

When we incorporate other ways to disseminate that information, and share it with thousands of people - instead of just one - those platforms create a magnet, which attracts *many customers.* In web-development lingo, this is referred to as 'developing a sticky web.'

I always encourage agents to transcribe all of the valuable information that's stored between their ears; this might include their experiences with new construction homes, new home buyers, bike trails around certain neighborhoods, sharing their culture, amazing marketing they execute, or different packages they offer. Through exploring these life and real estate experiences, and (most importantly) sharing them, agents will more quickly discover the true value behind their Unique Value Propositions.

Once captured, those unique experiences can be broadcast as 'sharable content' with more people, in a more efficient manner. In this sense, the book you're now reading is *my way* of practicing what I preach; putting down what I hope you will find to be valuable information, and creating many new and positive relationships as a result.

Once you've reconnected with your Natural Affinity Audience and identified the strongest tools in your toolkit, you'll have a better idea of how to compete to win in real estate, and increase your bottom line. You will no longer think of your Unique Value Proposition as merely 'Selling Real Estate.'

If you're still searching for your UVP, don't panic! Even when I teach smaller classes, which typically include around 30 agents, I often threaten to lock the door until *every one of them* has found their Unique Value Proposition. To date, everyone has escaped with at least one in hand - and *you will, too!*

Building Your Content Library - Marketing

As described above, your background *forms a framework* for great content that is unique to you. Content is a way to demonstrate your UVP, whether through a connection to something with the buyer or seller, or by providing content around a Program, which solves an issue for your client. When you build your library of content, it will be the gift that keeps on giving throughout your career.

Content is what you write, say, or visualize.

- Think of each blog post, email, video, and all communications as *chapters* in a book.

- Organize your thoughts into *topics*.

- Use the topics as tags on your blog, hash tags on your posts, and in the titles on your videos.

- *Organize your thoughts early on,* and your library of content will get more visits!

Example

Even content that does not form a UVP can be put to use in a powerful way.

If you've been in real estate for a while, think about the many questions you've been asked repeatedly. We know these as FAQs, or Frequently Asked Questions. Why not produce a FAQ sheet that can replace all of those elaborate emails you've sent to answer all of those important questions - yet still couldn't find 2 months later? This way, when someone else asks the same questions, you can locate your FAQ, and just hit 'Send!' In fact, whenever you're asked *any* question which you've already covered on your FAQ sheet, you can always refer to that FAQ as a script, or memory prompt.

Example

Later, as you build your team, your team members can refer and add to these documents, instead of them needing to start again from scratch. Consider all the time you've spent answering a common question, whether face-to-face, by phone, via email or text. Now imagine those answers being covered on *one page* (either your FAQ web page, published Google Doc, your Facebook Page, or YouTube video) and you'll realize that you're not only being more time-efficient, but making more valuable information available to many more potential buyers and sellers.

The idea here is to leverage and multiply the outcome of your hard work. Not only will you drive people to your content; when they search the topics you've covered, they will *also find you.*

When a client asks you a question - perhaps about underground storage tanks, the process of getting pre-approved, real estate tax rates or limits on renting out a condo unit - the subject matter will likely come up again at some point in your career. Instead of simply responding with an elaborate email covering your research, transcribe your research about this subject so that it can easily be posted, or published. Then you can point that buyer and others to the web page, or published page, etc.

It may take a little longer to hit 'file and publish' on your Google Doc, or web page. Still, since whatever you put down in writing must be correct anyways, won't your time spent researching the matter be the same? Sooner or later, other buyers and sellers will have a similar question; now you're only one click away from giving them the answer. Furthermore, now you'll be one of a very small number of agents who comes up in 'search results' for that topic. Capture more potential buyers and sellers by *extracting your knowledge* and presenting it online.

Example

As you can see, I like to leverage what I already know about as well as new things I learn along the way. Almost ten years into my real estate career, I'm still always learning something new. Even 'every-day business dealings' seem to generate new ideas for me, or my team, and often improve our bottom line.

- When my team has a 'lunch and learn' with an inspector or an appraiser, we capture our notes on a document for later use.

- When our agent representing a buyer shows a series of homes, and finds one that the buyer is not interested in - which may suit another buyer - they'll shoot a quick 'Walking-Tour Video' anyways, to share with their other signed buyers - and other agents representing buyers on the team.

- We publish a list of our buyers (without disclosing names) so sellers considering listing can match their home to our buyers. You can see an example of this at www.AllStarbuyers.com

There are many ways to set yourself apart as an agent, and that certainly includes looking more carefully at your marketing. What kind of marketing, specifically, sets *you apart?* What's different about what you offer? Perhaps you hold Open Houses that attract a crowd, by putting out 30+ signs and using an in-depth Program that works for you. Postcards, Newsletters, handwritten notes, blogs; the plethora of marketing options in real estate can be overwhelming. Choose one, and *learn about it in depth.* Squeeze all of the value from whichever works best for you.

Where can we find *content* for your UVP? Once we find it, how can we relate it to real estate, and monetize it where possible? This next section explores a framework to get you started.

Let's use the Facebook 'platform' as an example (which most agents frequently use) as well as some ideas to get started:

	Topics to post / collect (you can interchange blog with web page, depending on your ability)					
Mountain Biking (Interest)	Regular posts of pictures and trails	Link to your blog on in-depth maps	Link to your blog list of favor- ite bike shops	Link to blog on list of favorite online suppliers	Link to blog list of bik- ing groups in the area	Set up a Facebook page on Biking in XYZtown
Music (Interest / work experience)	Posts of you playing or at music events	Blog on schools with great Programs	Blog on favorite music shops in XYZ town	Visit music teachers in schools / indepen- dents and interview	Sponsor a music center or Program	Build a note into your corporate identity
B2C (Work Experience)	Make a list of offices and visit one per week, in your 'uniform'	Blog on your list and key attributes	Post regular pictures of your visits	Create a schedule for your visits so they get to know you	Write about your unique knowledge of the industry	Write about Programs that will help the audience

Building Block 3: Providing you with Programs that anticipate common real estate obstacles to success, before they happen.

Most often, you are competing for business. Your toolkit for success comprises your systems, tools, models and Programs. When you can define any of these in a unique way, it can become your Unique Value Proposition. As you learn to master that specific tool, you can bring in other ones. Note: these tools are especially valuable when prospecting for FSBOS (For Sale By Owners) and expired listings.

Take the tools you are using, flesh them out and clearly define them as a Program. You can see many examples of successful Programs used by my real estate network (AllStarCertified) in Chapter 2 of this book. Many Programs were designed with the following questions in mind:

- What is different about how I offer my services?

- What marketing Programs do I run that (most) others do not?

- What customer problems am I solving?

- What do customers and clients expect as a 'given,' - for example, better communication?

Useful Link

Hopefully, these sections provided a springboard for developing your Unique Value Proposition. If you'd like to spend more time honing in on your ideas, visit www.UVPBook.com and use our workbook to further develop your initial ideas.

If you have completed the companion workbook, choose 1-3 ideas that you think are the strongest, and note them down.

These are your three core ideas that made it through the '80% Rule.'

Applying The 'So What' rule

While honing in on your potential UVPs, take a hard look what at you're offering. Do they really operate by the 'So What' rule? Do people care? A great way to sort this out is to call a number of your 'forever clients' (called 'past' clients in traditional real estate) and ask them if they would find this Program or offering useful - or if they think others would. Note: we use the term 'forever clients,' because to my way of thinking, the term 'past clients' means 'they've gone away' ...or have died!

If you're creating a list for potential UVPs as you read this, you've likely run a few lines through your choices. **This is not a time to get deflated.** It just requires asking the right questions, to get down to what you are *really passionate* about. Most agents have to dig deep at this point. It's a new way of thinking - and it's surprising how hard it can be to determine where 'real estate' connects to what we're passionate about. Keep reading, as we find your magic!

Commission Cutting As A UVP

I'd suggest that identifying *commission* alone as a UVP is a poor differentiator. Consumers are interested in Value, and unless you've clearly differentiated your Value Proposition, they will regard *price* as your sole differentiator. You can do much better than this!

"IF VALUE IS NOT PRESENT OR MISUNDERSTOOD, PRICE MATTERS"

For example, the market is littered with 'limited service brokers,' i.e., firms that will list real estate at a low fee. Generally, 'limited service brokers' offer a sign, a lockbox for agents to show the home and a listing on the MLS. Occasionally, they will offer a menu of items that can be added, for a fee, in an 'a-la-carte' fashion. The value offered is generally much less than that of a full-service agent; however, if that same full-service agent is not clearly defining their value, they will indeed find it difficult to compete with those limited service brokers! These days it's hard for a consumer to truly determine the difference between all of the offerings, value-wise.

Chapter 2:

AllStarCertified's UVP Programs

T he following Programs define AllStarCertified agents' services to customers, and grew from a literal *obsession* with building our Unique Value Proposition. The Programs originated from my early days of finding ways to address customer issues, therefore passing the 'So What' Rule, and are now practiced by our exclusive AllStarCertified agent in each market. A handful of top agents offer a version of some of these programs around the country.

Each Program's core objective is to serve buyers or sellers at the highest level. This is accomplished by removing client issues and obstacles, including easing the real estate transaction itself. Our Programs address life circumstances as well, such as divorce and estate sales, which, without careful organization and management, can greatly complicate a real estate transaction.

Getting started with your own UVP really is an investment in the truest sense of the word. These programs were developed over the course of a decade, and running with *any one of these* will require both the time and energy needed to master the process and set up a system - which you then must manage. While some may choose to simply view this as 'extra work,'

"I WANT WHAT THEY'RE HAVING"

HOME SELLER

I view it as a longer-term investment, focused on running a value-based operation.

This extra effort consistently generates a better reputation, more referrals, and a wider, more active 'pipeline' of interest and activity in your operation. Short-term benefits include the 'lead-magnet effect' of the Programs to current prospective customers; when they're online (for example) and land on something *we're doing for a current client,* and think, "Wow. I want *what they're having."*

Not only do the Programs help attract and serve new clients, they also boost and support your 'forever clients,' or those you've already done business with. Top agents don't tend to base their prospecting on merely spending large amounts purchasing leads; rather they systematically 'follow up' and serve their forever clients, in order to earn their ongoing business. When often 80% of their business is attributed to (and driven by) referrals, it makes sense to focus on improving this aspect of one's business - something which all of these programs accomplish.

What Does That Mean For An Agent Team?

Tyler Elstrom has held many positions on a real estate team: Buyer agent, Listing agent, Operations Director, and he currently leads the AllStarCertified Network. In those previous roles, Tyler implemented the UVP programs outlined in this book, and now offers them (through the AllStarCertified network) to one agent in each Keller Williams Market Center.

"I'm going to be frank: coming on the team 5 years ago as a new agent, I was *skeptical.* The programs seemed like work, and I didn't understand some of them. I had a way of doing things that was easy and well-rehearsed. I believed heavily in the old saying 'If it isn't broke, don't fix it!' In short - I was not quick to change, and fought the work requirements involved.

Over the next 5 years, through trial and error I finally gained a better sense of the programs' value, and began incorporating them into my business. The funny thing is, all these years later I see this exact same pattern with the teams we collaborate with through the AllStarCertified Network.

At first, some are opposed. They give it their own spin; they will only use some of the programs, and not others - or they just ignore them completely! Then, during our weekly calls they raise certain situations (which the programs are designed solve), and we slowly integrate the programs. Eventually, whatever recurring issue they're experiencing always becomes 'resolved,' which speaks to how well the programs work.

Any model is great 'in theory' - but what if you take that model, and implement it in a completely different location - with different variables, circumstances, price points, market trends, and culture? In my position, I observed first-hand the impact these programs can have, ranging from a small town in North Dakota, to the hugely populated market of Atlanta, to an exclusive luxury market in Northern California. I've seen the programs implemented successfully by an individual agent, all the way up to a 20-person team. If I could go back in time to when I started, I'd go 'all in' on the programs, right away - and trade the headaches, days on market for my clients and all those appointments which I could have successfully converted *with having a stronger value proposition."*

Tyler Elstrom, www.AllStarCertified.com

Each Program section defines the Program itself, how it works and why we use it. The more complex Programs include scripts, and examples of how we present them to clients. Visit www.UVPBook.com to learn more about the complementary workbook available.

Before incorporating any of the following Programs, be sure to have any details reviewed by your local attorney, as laws can (and do) vary from state to state!

An Overview Of The Programs

Program 1: AllStar Love It Or Leave It Program™

Program 2: Homes for Heroes - a Program of Giving

Program 3: AllStar Certified Pre-Owned™ (CPO): AllStar CPO™

Program 4: Bringing A Listing To Life - AllStar Listing Storyboard™

Program 5: Walking-Tour Videos - AllStar Walking Tour™

Program 6: Coming Soon - AllStar Coming Soon™

Program 7: Radio and Education Programs for sellers and buyers

Program 8: Priority Seller and Buyer

Program 9: Sell For Free Buy New

Program 10: Land Sales Packages

Program 11: AllStar Lease Option™

Program 12: AllStar Estate Planning™ Program

Program 13: AllStar Divorce Real Estate Planning™ Program

Program 14: Referrals

Program 15: Providing The Highest Level Of Service For Clients

Program 1: Love It Or Leave It Guarantee - AllStar Love It Or Leave It Program™

Definition

The Love It or Leave It Guarantee Program **addresses** the issue of a buyer being in the uncomfortable position of having to make a sudden change during the first 6 months of ownership. It provides for *a no-cost sale* (on the seller side) during the first six months after clients purchase a home from an agent offering the Program. When a buyer has purchased a home from any AllStarCertified.com agents operating this Program, that agent will sell it for free for the first six months of ownership - and at a discount after that - which continues for up to ten years after purchasing the home. The Program is also attractive to home sellers, as it is going to attract more buyers.

Typical Objection

"I Can't Go Around Selling Homes For Free"

Initially, agents may be nervous about offering the Love It Or Leave It Guarantee, often saying, "I can't go around selling homes for free."

The fact is, most people aren't going to turn around and sell their home in the first six months. In almost a decade of my team buying and selling with over 1300+ sales, this has only happened once. Still, if the client has no choice, and must sell, do you really want to insist that someone in this difficult situation *pay you that commission?* If the buyer has to sell the

Scenario

home soon after they bought it, there will not likely be any gain in value. Not only that - they'll now have to pay commission to an agent.

- Tom buys a $500,000 home in January with an agent offering the Program.

- In March, he learns that his mom has a severe illness, and wishes to assist his father with her care, in a different state.

- Tom now needs to sell his new home.

- Tom paid $500,000 three months ago, and the home's value has not increased.

- His agent charges 6% to sell the home. He lists the home at $500,000, and will pay $30,000 in commission.

- His Listing agent will pay $15,000 of that commission to the agent representing the buyer.

- The AllStar Love It Or Leave It Program covers the $15,000 that would be paid to the Listing agent, when the home is part of the **CPO Program.**

That's where our AllStar Certified Pre-Owned Program (CPO) comes into play. One of the elements of CPO verifies the home's value through an Appraisal. In the above scenario, the value of Tom's property has remained the same. However, in other cases, the property's value may either increase or decrease. Once we determine *true market value* of the property through CPO, we will then sell it for him, for free, at no cost (on the seller side).

Learn More

See CPO Program.

Why We Offer The Love It Or Leave It Guarantee.

Life happens! Once in a great while, especially in today's world, after someone makes one of the largest investments in their life, the purchaser may have to turn around and sell it way too soon, perhaps due to a family illness or job promotion. Why offer the Guarantee? Simply stated, it doesn't seem right that someone who's struggling with something so difficult should have to pay for the same thing, twice. For a buyer going into a purchase, *that alone* can really give peace of mind.

How The AllStar Love It Or Leave It Program Came About

The Program was born from an experience I had early in my real estate career. I had a client whose parents were aging, and one of them was experiencing health difficulties. Therefore, my client wanted to move back to his home state to be with them, in case something happened. He knew that in this manner, he could offer them more support on a daily basis - which was understandable.

When these types of situations occur, it's usually the result of one of five things:

- A Job promotion or Job loss.
- An accident that causes a disability.
- Wanting to be with grandkids, after the kids themselves move away.
- Parents, or someone they are close to, are located elsewhere and need help.
- A life-changing event, such as a pregnancy or death in the family.

How Our AllStar Love It Or Leave It Program
Appears Online And In Print:

AllStarCertified agents understand that purchasing real estate will likely be among our client's most significant financial investments. We created our Ten Year 'AllStar Love it or Leave it' Program to give you even more peace of mind - and it's the most generous guarantee in the business!

Our team of handpicked professionals are trained to listen, and are dedicated to finding the "Perfect Home" for you. That's why we are willing to work for Free* if your new home isn't everything you expected it to be, or if circumstances such as change of employment or family emergencies occur.

* Free or reductions are applied to the seller-side of the commission only, as the agent representing the buyer will expect their share of the commission. It is also applied after any other costs such as referral fees. You must use our CPO Program to benefit from the discounted or free status, and allow us to refer you to a top agent in the area you are moving to (should you be moving out of the area).

Love It Or Leave It Time-line:

- **First Six Months after closing day**

  Should you need to sell your home for any reason, we will SELL IT FOR FREE*

- **6 Months - 2 years After Closing Day**

  We will sell your home for a .3% reduction of the selling side commission. Contact us for a full outline of our commission structure.

- **2-10 Years after Closing Day**

  We will sell your home for a .2% reduction of the selling side commission. Contact us for a full outline of our commission structure.

Key Benefits

Key benefits of the program: *The Love Or Leave It Guarantee Assists:*

- Buyers who need to turn around and sell their home, due to an unforeseen circumstance.

- Sellers and agents who wish to attract more buyers to their listed home, removing some of the 'buyer anxiety', which causes them to 'sit on the fence.'

- Agents who wish to provide more value in their quarterly calls to forever clients, i.e., *"don't forget our Love It Or Leave It Program."*

Featured Agent

Holli McCray's The Holli McCray Group, Knoxville, TN uses her Love it Or Leave It guarantee to great effect. Holli explains:

"Believe it or not, very few of our buyer clients have used our guarantee. We credit this low number to our expert buyer agent team, because they're putting our clients in the right house, at the right time. That said, we know that people's circumstances can change in an instant, and when they do, we want our clients to know that we have their backs! Having a happy client for life who refers his or her friends to us is worth more than any single transaction commission."

Program 2: Homes For Heroes:
A Program of Giving

Definition

Homes for Heroes® is the largest nationwide network of affiliate real estate specialists and local business affiliates committed to providing easy ways for the heroes of our nation to save on a home, and on every day home-related purchases. Shortly after 9/11, Homes for Heroes was established to give back to firefighters, law enforcement, military (active, reserves & veterans), healthcare workers, EMS and teachers for all they do. The Hero Rewards® check they receive for using the program is our way to say "Thank you."

How it works: Homes for Heroes affiliate partners pay an annual membership fee plus a 30% referral fee on hero closings. When a hero buyer uses the Homes for Heroes program they receive, post-closing, a *Hero Rewards check equal to .7% of the purchase price. Hero sellers receive a commission credit, at closing. Through the participation of the affiliated real estate professionals, as of May 2017, the program has served more than 15,000 heroes with more than $22 million dollars in Hero Rewards, on more than $1 billion in hero real estate volume. Additionally, Homes for Heroes also serves heroes in need through its private foundation and corporate giving program. Real estate professionals grow their business, heroes receive Hero Rewards on their real estate transaction AND heroes who are in need are served. It is truly a circle of giving.

For complete information on the Homes for Heroes program, visit www. HomesForHeroes.com

* Dollar amounts are estimates and are limited and/or restricted in AK, KS, LA, and MS. You must be enrolled with Homes for Heroes and be represented at closing by a Homes for Heroes affiliate real estate specialist to be eligible.

Why We Use Homes For Heroes

I came across Homes for Heroes while designing a similar Program (to use locally) - and found that Ruth Johnson's 'Homes for Heroes' was already in place, and organized across the nation.

"I've worked in the real estate industry for nearly 40 years. I know real estate, and I'm pretty good at it. I believe Rowena is cut from the same professional fabric. She knew that her experience and talent could build a successful and thriving business.

Sometimes, out of tragedy, life takes you in a different direction than you intended to go in. This happened to me shortly after 9/11, when all of us were dealing with the effects of that terrible day. My son came into my office and said, "we should give back to those who give so much, and we should call it "Homes for Heroes." This became my new personal and professional direction.

Like me, I believe there came a point in Rowena's career where she felt her experience and talent could positively impact her community even further, and that led her to Homes for Heroes. Rowena joined Homes for Heroes as an affiliate real estate partner in 2011. Since 2013, she has been in the top 1% out of more than 2,200 affiliates and has given back to over 250 heroes in her market. I could not be more proud of her, and all she's done for her local heroes - and in furthering the success of Homes for Heroes.

Homes for Heroes went from being a local effort to a nationwide Program in 2009. To date, the Program has served more than 15,000 heroes with more than $22 million dollars in savings on their real estate transactions. Find out more at www.HomesForHeroes.com."

Ruth Johnson, CEO Homes for Heroes

How Homes For Heroes Came About

Ruth's commendable work with Homes for Heroes is an inspiration, and her kind words towards me don't just lie at my door. Thanks goes to *all agents* who give up part of their earnings on every Homes for Heroes transaction they handle - and the community servers who do so much for us!

At the Asheville, NC AllStar Headquarters, agents have given back over $550,000 to those who serve our nation and its communities: firefighters, law enforcement, military (active, reserves & veterans), healthcare workers, EMS and teachers. We're on a continuing mission to give back $1,000,000, *as soon as possible.* It's a very popular Program which has become about a third of the Asheville, NC head-quarter's business.

These *community heroes* are giving so much, and working such long hours - and way too often, putting their lives at risk - that it's really just a small way to say 'thank you,' and to give back. It's very rewarding, and all real estate professionals in the program appreciate having an avenue to show their appreciation.

Typical Homes For Heroes Script

The following is an illustration of how 'Homes for Heroes' works, through a conversation with either a home seller, or a home buyer.

Script

Agent to buyers or sellers:
Mr. buyer / Mrs. seller, I noticed that you have an .edu in your email address, are you a teacher?

(Or)

Sir, what do you do for a living? We have a Program where, because of our participation, you can receive Hero Rewards as a "thank you" for all that you do. Firefighters, law enforcement, military (active, reserves & veterans), healthcare workers, EMS and teachers all qualify and the Hero Rewards are substantial - with an average over $1,500.

Buyer/seller:
What's the catch?

Agent:
(Chuckle) I can understand why you would think there is one! All we have to do is have a copy of your license or badge number.

Buyer/seller:
Wow, I've never heard of agents giving money back to the community like this.

Agent: (Insert your figures)

We've given back over $550,000 to local community servers so far, and aim to get to one million dollars as quickly as possible. Can you help?

Starting Your Giving Program

If you're just starting the Program, your conversation with sellers and buyers will be about why you're passionate about giving back to local community servers. If you can tie in some personal stories about how they've made a strong impression, or helped you at some point in your life, even better! If you're already one of the over 2,200+ real estate professional in Homes For Heroes, or a similar Program, then use the amount which you (or other agents in the Program) have already given back. *Note: the amount is less important that the fact that you have given! After all, the more people who learn about the Program through your giving, the more people *will be helped in the future.* Key thought here: it's all about the *'thank you!'*

Key Benefits

Key Benefits Of The Program: *Homes For Heroes Assists:*

- Buyers in the qualifying professions who get 25% back from the agent's commission, as a check, after closing.

- Sellers who get a reduction in listing commission.

- Agents who wish to support their local community through an established program, without building their own.

There are so many ways to give; Homes for Heroes is just one. What groups are you interested in supporting?

 **Featured Agent**

Ashley Wilson, agent in Raleigh, NC, gives back through her charitable organization, the Triangle Spokes Group, (est. 2006), an organization that distributes *new bicycles and helmets* to less fortunate families. 100% of the donations go towards the bikes and helmets, with operating expenses covered by the co-founders of the organization, Ashley Wilson and Jenn Nowalk. They partner with the Salvation Army in Wake County to distribute the bicycles in time for the holiday season, and since inception have given away 4,450 bikes.

To give you an idea of the numbers, Wake County expected over 4,000 families and 9,000 children to come to them for help in 2016. Ashley says, "The quintessential gift to receive on Christmas morning for children of all ages has been a shiny new bike. Triangle Spokes Group is excited about the idea of carrying on this tradition in the Triangle, and making the holidays brighter for local children."

For more information, visit: www.trianglespokesgroup.org

 **Featured Agent**

Kristan Cole is a top Agent and Vice-President of Expansion for Keller Williams. She supports her daughter's mission to provide helmets to those who cannot afford them, as well as many other causes.

Kristan and her family originally hail from Alaska, where, as in many other rural areas, ATVs are the vehicle of choice - especially for youths.

Unfortunately, hospitalization or death from traumatic brain injuries is also 10 percent higher among Alaska residents than the national average.

Kristan's daughter, Teagen Tanner founded "Helmets On Heads" after she herself experienced a critical ATV accident in Homer, Alaska. In 2015, as a passenger on a short, low-speed ATV ride on uneven terrain, Teagen and her ATV rolled over. As Teagen was not wearing a helmet, she almost lost her life. While she made an astounding recovery, she still suffered from a brain injury, and bears the scars on her face to this day. One month after this experience, Teagen was driven to start "Helmets On Heads."

71% of the time helmets are proven effective in preventing brain injury, and death. The nonprofit "Helmets On Heads" reinforces a 'culture of safety' by raising awareness about the importance of helmet safety and providing helmets to those who need, yet can't afford them. Teagen's nonprofit warehouses helmets designed for all types of activities - and her vision is to build the program around the country!

To find out more information, or to make a donation, visit www.HelmetsOnHeads.com.

 **Featured Agent**

Nick Shivers is a Portland, OR agent who gives back through a charitable organization he founded 10 years ago, in Nicaragua. "Sell a Home, Save a Child" helps children in Nicaragua, Mexico, Haiti, and Kenya, through monthly memberships of $250 - $750 a month, donated by agents (or others) in the real estate industry. So far, the organization has raised over $600,000. Find out more at www.sellahomesaveachild.org

 **Featured Agent**

Adrienne Lally and Attilio Leonardi, Brokers of Team Lally - Hawaii's #1 Real Estate Team, combats child homelessness through their charitable program, 'Sell A Home Save A Keiki.' For every home sold through Team Lally, a portion of the commission will go toward putting a homeless child in one of their own.

Partnering with Project Hawaii Inc., Team Lally helps provide summer camps, rehabilitative programs, food and major necessities not easily accessible to homeless children. While donating a portion of their commissions year-round, 'Sell A Home Save A Keiki' also hosts canned food drives, a Christmas Fund-raiser and many more events throughout the year to combat the serious issue of homeless children.

Keep up with the "Sell A Home Save A Keiki" movement at www. SellAHomeSaveAKeiki.com

Program 3: AllStar Certified Pre-Owned™ (CPO): The Listing Of The Future - AllStar CPO™

What Is Certified Pre-Owned? A Review In Real Estate Common Sense.

A CPO home comprises three main elements, which include the following:

Definition

1. Up-front Appraisal

The professional appraisal provides an objective, dependable price for the home, and replaces the traditional CMA, which is often produced by agents of differing abilities and perspectives.

2. Up-front Inspections

Any items that come up on the pre-listing inspection are taken care of by the seller, on the seller's terms. This reduces the chance of stressful, last minute negotiations that often occur once the home is under contract - and can result in a buyer easily walking out on that contract.

3. Home Warranty

The home warranty covers repair of many units, systems and their components that frequently break down and need repair during the first, expensive year of ownership.

Once these three elements are implemented, the buyer is now purchasing a home that (1) has a professional market value via the Appraisal, (2) has no known issues and (3) will be covered, should issues occur during the first year of ownership.

Why We Developed The CPO Listing

CPO *puts the seller in the driver's seat,* by addressing and removing roadblocks which almost always show up during the average contract negotiation. This becomes especially important to sellers once they realize that *up to one-third of contracts fail.* Once a property goes under contract, it is essentially off the market - and at that point, few buyers, if any, are considering it. Should a contract fail, that valuable sales time has been wasted. In addition, a home which failed to close can, and often does develop a 'stigma' in the eyes of other potential buyers, who may ask themselves - and their agent - why that contract failed!

The CPO process results in a higher probability of the property being sold, while reducing stress during the transaction for all parties. To understand how it works, it's helpful to revisit what happens during an *average traditional real estate transaction*:

Traditional Real Estate Scenario

Note: some 'scenarios' may differ from state to state; this one is simply provided as an example, for the purpose of discussion:

Scenario

1. The property is listed once an agent advises a seller of a fair market price. This is usually accomplished through a tool called a CMA, or Comparable Market Analysis.

2. An agent representing the buyer (sometimes the Listing agent) presents an offer to the seller.

3. The agent/s go back and forth, brokering the agreement. At this point, there is no knowledge of what repairs may be needed (if any), or whether the home will appraise for a loan, or appraise to the satisfaction of a cash-paying buyer.

4. Once a contract is ratified, the agent/s then help the buyer arrange an inspection on the home, usually within the first couple of weeks.

5. The buyer's agent helps the buyer with funding for the home (often through a bank or other lending institution) or with preparation of a 'proof of funds' letter for cash-paying buyers.

6. The inspection report comes back, typically with an average of 25+ items that 'need repair.'

7. The agent/s go back and forth, re-brokering the agreement, depending on which items the seller agrees to repair. The seller may be willing to give to the buyer a credit to repair the items themselves. Should the seller not agree to do the repairs, the common figure that the agent representing the buyer suggests for a credit against the purchase price is $2,000 - $2,500.

8. At this point in the re-negotiation, in many US states, the buyer can choose to exit the contract. (Sometimes, a 'due diligence fee'

which the buyer has paid is non-refundable - however, most often the 'earnest money' which the buyer has paid is refundable).

9. The lending institution gets all necessary documentation from the buyers (as many buyers do not supply this up-front) and decides what loan amount they will offer. An Appraisal is then ordered to ascertain the appraiser's opinion of price. (Homes do not always appraise for what the property is listed at; in a market where prices are flat or on the decline, this is not uncommon). Most Appraisals are going to come in 21-30 days after the contract is signed, and sometimes even later.

10. If the property does not appraise for the price on the contract, the agent/s go back and forth, re-brokering the agreement.

11. Up to one third of contracts fall apart at this stage.

    a. Buyers may get nervous with the amount of things that need repair.

    b. If the property does not appraise, an extra dose of 'buyer nerves' gets thrown in.

    c. Should the buyers decide to pull out (and the choice is most often the buyer's) they have the following invested: any due diligence fee, the inspection fees (usually $350-$650) and a potential fee for the loan application.

    d. Earnest money is often refundable at this stage.

*Again, check with your state for the elements on the purchase contract.

As you can see, negotiations often occur *at least three times* before the buyers are handed the keys to the property:

1. During the agreement of the **original contract**, when buyers have found the home of their dreams - and the sellers are excited to get a contract (an important note)!

2. **Inspections**. *Note - In the 1300+ transactions the AllStarCertified team (at the Asheville NC headquarters) has handled to date, we haven't once seen an inspection report with less than ten items on it that need repair - unless they have followed the CPO Process).

3. **Appraisals**. Should the property not appraise, the buyers and sellers are thrust back into negotiations.

These hurdles are not the only ones to a real estate transaction, however they are the *main ones*. The CPO process changes the way that real estate is transacted, for the benefit of both the buyer and the sellers.

How CPO came about

The seeds of the AllStar Certified Pre-Owned Program were sown just before I became a licensed agent, and was purchasing and selling property. In 2006, we were on the verge of the looming sub prime mortgage crisis, and the prices in most markets had begun falling from their high point. This meant that sellers were just as concerned about selling their home as buyers were about purchasing them; both were wondering how much money their homes would quickly lose in value.

I was marketing to various neighborhoods, including my own, in order to attract listings. While the listings were coming in hard and fast, simple 'CMA's were no longer convincing sellers of current market conditions. Buyers were starting to get edgy - and perhaps, rightfully so. Everyone involved was operating in an environment where *trusting the price* was critical.

This environment led to me ask every seller to have an Appraisal completed *before* I listed the home, so we could establish its *true market value,* which could then be attached to the MLS (to underpin that value). Which is exactly what I proceeded to do! -Sure enough, I soon received calls and questions from agents in my market, asking *'why was I attaching Appraisals to the MLS?'* To which I often replied, " I'm not publishing their 'inside leg measurements...' *just the market value of the home,* along with accurate dimensions, and a floor plan!"

At the time, my decision to request that every seller have an Appraisal did feel somewhat risky. Still, it was a *calculated risk,* which assumed that 50% of the sellers would say 'no,' and the other 50% would agree to it. When almost all of my clients said "yes," I was pleasantly surprised. They quickly understood the value of having the Appraisal, and soon after that, the idea became a 'no-brainer.' The approach not only gave clients more confidence 'going in,' it also had the added benefit of *being different* - a welcomed change in the real estate environment, where things had been done *the same way, for so long.*

The CPO Program grew from this pre-Appraisal process. I would later add an up-front inspection and Home Warranty to the property's marketing, with very positive results. If sellers or a listing agent do not decide to invest in the CPO process immediately, and the home is still for sale, the 'reverse' CPO Program can be very useful in 'freshening' the listing - and will often result in a much faster sale. Sellers are often more willing to engage in the process when their home has not sold.

How The CPO Program Works

Let's look at each element in more detail:

Element 1: The Appraisal

Definition

CPO agents' process begins with an agent contacting an appraiser (on behalf of the seller) to appraise the house before listing, or as soon as the paperwork is signed. As you will see, the Appraisal puts the seller in the driving seat, as they'll have a better representation of the true market value; the home is neither overpriced, nor under priced. It's at *correct market value.*

Sometimes, sellers might say, "Oh, I've had a refinancing, or 'refi Appraisal' and I wasn't happy with it." However, a refinancing Appraisal is designed for a different purpose than a marketing Appraisal - and it often isn't current. Any appraiser will tell you that appraising is an Art, not a Science. More correctly, Appraisers follow scientific procedures required by their profession, and then render a final opinion of price using their personal judgment.

Most sellers are pleasantly surprised at the value their home comes in at. CPO agents tell the sellers that *there is no commitment to list the house at that price.* In fact, we caution that the Appraisal is between the seller and the Appraiser, and if for any reason they are not happy with it, they can slip it in a drawer and we will not discuss it further - though this rarely happens.

The Appraisal As Part Of The Traditional Real Estate Scenario

CMAs (Current Market Analysis) are traditionally how agents price houses. A great CMA is a wonderful thing to behold - however, many CMAs are nuts! There, *I said it!* The truth is, no two agents are alike when it comes to the *skills required to produce them.* Here's why I feel that way:

1. Sometimes, a real estate agent will come in and say, "Your house should be listed at $500,000, and here's why." However, the seller

     may (and often will) attempt to *force their opinion,* as they 'need to get $X out of the home.'

2.   An agent's ability to 'price properly' ranges from 'poor' to 'great.' Seller's homes are often their biggest asset, and yet having some agent pressing a button on the MLS (Multiple Listing Service) - the 'quick way' to price a home without a 'real person' analyzing the data - often leads to disaster. The result is similar to an automated online valuation, offered by many of the vendors whose business model is to sell leads to agents. Contrast this with an Appraisal, where a professional takes 6 hours or more to appraise a home.

3.   When agents price a listing, it is (at that point) with total disregard to what inspection items need repairing. Sellers often believe that there's nothing really wrong with their home - yet on average, when the inspection is over, there are more than 25 items that need repairing. Often, they include some nit-picky things that can easily be taken care of. So when these items are addressed up-front, CPO soon becomes a compelling argument as to why this is *the right way* to adjust the process. It's just insanity to put a home on the market without knowing what's wrong with it, or knowing what an appraiser will find to be its market value. For that reason, I created the **AllStar Certified Pre-Owned Program** for our sellers and buyers.

Why We Use The Up-front Appraisal Approach

Once the property goes under contract, everyone's excited. The sellers think, "Finally, *my house is sold.*"

The buyers think, "At last, we've found our perfect home." I've asked agents from around the country to share their thoughts on why one-third of contracts either 'drop-out,' or go under contract - *and then fail to close?* Two main reasons which always come up point to *the Inspection,* and *the Appraisal* - when and how they are executed - *and why.*

Buyers' Unfamiliarity With Market Conditions

Prices go up and down, depending on market conditions. Frequently, buyers are not moving to the next street, or even the same town. They are not familiar with their destination, and therefore, its *local values*. Buyers (and agents representing the buyers) can do a great deal of research, yet that won't inspire the confidence an Appraisal will. Appraisers spend an average of 6 hours appraising a house; they will provide a more reliable value. It's their primary job. Appraising is all they do, every day.

An Appraisal Can Identify Which Remodeling Or Repair Will Bring The Most Return

An added benefit is that many appraisers will do the Appraisal *based on work that will be done to* prepare for sale (for example, refinishing floors, remodeling the kitchen, adding a bathroom, etc.). Some sellers may finish out the 'bonus room' over the garage - others may finish the basement, investing in additional living space because it's going to increase the square footage.

One issue is that the additional living space (or other improvements) may not provide the best return on the investment they make. Most basements are not going to appraise at the same value per square foot as the space counted as 'main-level living.'

Second, that enlarged home may now be the biggest in the neighborhood, a process known as 'Over Improving.' Homes are appraised using the homes that are *most similar to the subject home.* Sellers are wise to ask the appraiser, "if I will improve this, what difference will there be in the value?" Most appraisers will provide that information. In these cases, the seller can make a more informed decision about moving forward with any repairs *before making them.*

Element 2: The 'up-front' Inspection

Definition

In a traditional inspection, an inspection is performed on a home when it is under contract, paid for by the buyer, usually within the first fourteen days after a contract is ratified. In an 'up-front' inspection, the home is inspected *before it is listed on the MLS,* and paid for by the seller. This removes the 'unknown' items that usually need repairing on a home, or need further investigation - 25 of them, on average - that come up after the home is under contract. The up-front inspection fees ($350+) are usually recouped *many times over.* But it does *more than that,* as you will see!

You may be familiar with the concept of CPO offered by car manufacturers. Car companies offer the Certified Pre-Owned approach that offers something like a 150+ point inspection for $20,000 cars. Why do we think it's 'normal' to market a $200,000+ home without offering a 'pre-inspection?' Or pricing a home based on 'what we've put in it?' We've been doing it that way for so long now, that it's rarely questioned - though it should be.

Since most sellers don't thoroughly prepare their homes for sale, the contract is *designed to provide protections to the buyer.* Providing for an up-front Inspection effectively puts the seller *back in the driver's seat,* and re-balances the relationship.

Let's compare the up-front inspection process with the inspection being performed later, in a traditional contract:

When an AllStarCertified agent gets an offer on one of the CPO listings, we know it's pretty much smooth sailing, and many more of these homes actually sell. **The up-front inspection** process is more attractive to all parties, because:

- Even though the buyers sometimes still choose to get their own inspection, there'll be very few items on the inspection report that need repair - and often none. Any experienced agent representing the buyer will say 'it's among the cleanest inspections they've ever seen' - so the buyers will feel more comfortable.

- The buyers see the Appraisal, which lists all the square footage, as well as a floor plan with all the square footage detailed on it. They know that what they are paying (per square foot of home) is accurate, according to market value.

- The home will likely appraise, as there is already an Appraisal in place.

In a 'traditional' contract, when the inspection is done during the contract period:

- When swayed by the results of the inspection or Appraisal, the buyer can walk out on the contract fairly easily, with little or no money out-of-pocket (other than money spent on the inspection report). When the inspection takes place, and the report comes back, the seller and buyer are essentially renegotiating the contract. If the seller does the pre-listing inspection, any of the 25+ items that arise can be addressed. Often, a handy-person can take care of the minimal items - or even the homeowner. In some states, however, when the home is under contract, the repairs have to be done by a licensed professional. Check with your local real estate commission as to whether that's a regulation or not in your area. -Even if that's not a real estate commission regulation, wouldn't you (as a buyer) *insist* on a licensed contractor?

- There's another key issue which can derail negotiations during the contract phase - the *buyer tends to wield the power.* They may say, "I want these repairs done by a licensed contractor. I want them done one week before we close - so we can inspect everything again - and make sure every thing's okay."

Now, what do you think happens to *the price of repair,* now that *all items must be completed in a short period of time* - and those contractors know it? It causes stress. However, when agents help the sellers take care of issues up-front, there is the luxury of time for more exploration of the issues and how to resolve them.

- Quotations and estimates can be gathered for any larger items. Let's say something on the roof needs fixing (*a classic*)! Perhaps it's flashing around the chimney that needs some attention. It's relatively inexpensive, however costs enough to require some quotes. Now, the seller can save money by gathering quotes, and choosing the right contractor for them. Contrast that with a 'repair request' during a traditional transaction, when everyone's stressed out and anxieties are high.

Let's consider the mindset of the seller when the home is under contract.

When a seller finally makes the decision to sell their house, they are generally excited, as they are moving on to the next phase of their lives. Maybe they are moving to be close to the grandkids in Arizona, moving for a new job, 'right-sizing' from their family home or have a new baby on the way. With an up-front inspection, the sellers, buyers and agents are much more confident that they'll actually go to the closing table. For those who are sad to leave their home, see AllStar Memories Video Program.

In contrast, with a traditional waiting period for the inspection, everyone's on pins and needles, waiting to see what will be wrong with the home. Sleepless nights are often the result - which can translate to *The Beginning of The End.* Add to this that (on average) the agent representing the buyer (and the buyer) will be asking for somewhere between $2,000 and $2,500 for the repairs.

What's the seller likely to do at that stage? Everybody knows that the seller is likely to be open to negotiation, because at this stage, sellers often feel like they're over a barrel. *More stress!* Again, as in so many operational areas of business, we often don't think much about what happens, or why - because it's '*just the way it's always been done.*'

61

Ask yourself: *in which mindset do you think the seller would make a better decision?*

CPO And Traditional Scenario: Comparison of Costs Involved

Traditional Process:

Scenario

- The buyer wants $2,500 off the price of the home, for repairs.

- The seller negotiates the amount down to $2,000.

- Buyers sometimes leave the contract, questioning what else has not been maintained.

- Cost of the stress involved?

CPO Process:

- Seller spends $350 to $450 to have the inspection done up-front.

- On average, cost will be $200 or $300 to get a handy-person to fix everything. (Now in some states a licensed contractor will be required to do this, so check with state regulators beforehand).

- Approximately $700 for the inspection and the repairs (of course, this can vary).

Even if your state requires the use of licensed contractors up-front, the seller may be able to take care of some of the items themselves. For example, the squeaking hinge on a cabinet door, in the kitchen. Now, if it's a bigger item, they'll want to use a licensed contractor anyway.

Sellers May Choose To Disclose Issues Instead Of Fixing Them

Let's look at this scenario.

1. In a CPO transaction, a buyer looks at a house wherein the seller disclosed that according to the inspection, the furnace is 15 years

old, and may need replacing in the next 2 years. *The sellers had an up-front Inspection, didn't have any money to fix any items, and chose to disclose the issues.*

2. *In a traditional transaction,* the buyer and seller (in the above example) *may have no idea* about the issues. The seller sets the price on the home not taking into account the issues that haven't yet been discovered. The buyer makes an offer on the house, with no knowledge of the condition.

As a buyer, or agent representing the buyer, which transaction would you be more comfortable with? In the CPO transaction, items are disclosed up-front, and all parties are negotiating on a property *'eyes wide-open.'*

Getting The Up-front Inspection On The Home

The next stage is getting the home inspected before listing it on the MLS. Some agents choose to list, and get the inspection underway immediately, so as not to hold up the listing going on the MLS. Agents can consider

Learn More

using it in conjunction with the Coming Soon Program in order to list the home as 'coming soon', while the inspections and Appraisal are carried out.

See Coming Soon Program.

Element 3: What is 'The Home Warranty?'

Definition

The home warranty completes the CPO trifecta. It is not the same as a home insurance plan. It's generally defined as a service contract that covers home system components, and systems when they break down due to normal wear and tear. Every Home Warranty Company offers a list of the items that are covered, which differ depending on the company. Typical coverage includes kitchen appliances, the electrical system, the plumbing system and central heating. Most companies will offer additional coverage, including things like the ice-maker on the refrigerator, for an extra fee.

In a traditional scenario, we already know that the agent representing the buyer commonly requests home warranties. It can add yet another thing to consider in the negotiation. The seller has not been able to market the home as offering a home warranty.

Scenario

In a CPO scenario, buyers know that home has been inspected, and that *there is an Appraisal* offered as part of the deal. The home warranty raises the buyers' peace of mind and comfort level for at least a year, once they buy the home.

Additional Benefit Of Coverage For Sellers

Make sure that your Home Warranty Company offers a good seller's warranty. This is a warranty which the company offers the seller for free during the listing period. Some home warranty companies put a time limit on that offer - often 6 months. The seller will usually pay call-out fees. There may also be a cap on the maximum payout to the seller. Be sure to set clear expectations with your sellers about how 'the home warranty being free to them' works. Although a home warranty for the seller over the listing duration may seem free, it's important for them to know what its limitations might be. For example - if it doesn't cover the AC, and other items that may only be offered in a 'platinum' package - then let your sellers know up-front. Sellers pay for the warranty when it is transferred to the buyers at closing.

Homes Sell Faster And For More Money

American Home Shield, one of the largest Home Warranty providers, released data that shows that one of their home warranties will help you sell your home an average of 11 days faster - and for an average or $2,314 more.* The average warranty costs between $350 - $600 (and more for additional, or specific items). It's worth doing your research on these, and checking reviews in your market.

Based on data collected by AHS and a large national real estate firm of the firm's listings that closed between January 1, 2012 and December 31, 2012.

AHS studied 24,230 listings from across the country ranging in price from $100,000 to $500,000. Cannon & Company, a third-party accounting firm, verified these results.

Typical CPO SCRIPT

Most agents probably realize that many home sellers have little experience or knowledge regarding *what really occurs* once a home goes under contract. Other than the basics of a contract being presented, an inspection taking place and the closing (where documents are signed and keys are handed over), *what takes place in-between those transactions can be confounding!* The below exchanges (in script format) were designed to highlight the advantages of 'the CPO approach' vs. 'what happens during an old-fashioned transaction' during a listing appointment - and identify key reasons why the 'CPO approach' provides the greater value.

Here's how CPO is presented at an AllStarCertified listing appointment, which includes the following characters:

a. *Listing agent* using the CPO Program (representing the sellers)

Script

b. *The home sellers*, Mr. and Mrs. Jones

c. *Traditional buyer's agent*, Gladys.

:

After pleasantries with the home sellers (Mr. and Mrs. Jones) the CPO agent gets down to the business of explaining how the 'CPO process' *changes the whole transaction for the better* - especially when compared to traditional ways of doing things.

Scenario

All dialogue is italicized. -

'Notes To Reader' are in bold.

CPO agent begins addressing the home sellers:

Mr. and Mrs. Jones, the good news is that I sell more homes than anyone in this area. Therefore, I'm the agent that will get your home sold. One of the main reasons this will happen is because years ago, my group made a decision to step out of the 'old-fashioned real estate process,' and into a better way of proceeding with real estate transactions.

Q: Do you know what the 2 main hurdles in a real estate sale are?

(CPO agent waits - silence - and then answers)

A: The Appraisal and the Inspection.
-Let me show you how we deal with those hurdles up-front, to save you hassle, stress, time and money. We refer to this as our CPO or AllStar Certified Pre-Owned Program.

An 'old-fashioned approach' to your home sale would have begun with an agent representing the buyer bringing the offer to the listing agent. Let's name her 'Gladys.' The conversation between the agents would (typically) go something like this: "Thank you very much for the offer, Gladys - please help me understand why it's such a low - ball offer, though?'

Gladys usually starts off low; because that's the way it's always been done. - (You've probably heard this before, haven't you)?

At this point, most sellers are aware of low-ball offers, and will tell the agent 'their own' story about 'low-ball offers.' They'll vent about 'what happened during their expired listing, when they got a 'ridiculously low' offer - or what happened to their sister in Arkansas...' etc. (We've all been there).

The CPO agent continues with:

Mr. and Mrs. Jones, often, after the 'low-ball' discussion, this conversation soon follows -

Gladys, the agent representing the buyers says:
Well, I did my CMA, (that's the comparable market analysis, a basic model of valuation).

And -

In 'old-fashioned real estate,' the listing agent would normally respond with:
-Well, I did my CMA too, thank you very much!

Then,

Gladys counters with:
My CMA is better than your CMA.
The listing agent replies, why is your CMA better?

The two agents then debate about the value. "I can't believe you used that home with the blue door as a comparable sale... (etc.)"

(In other words, the two agents are bantering back and forth, yet neither is able to really gain any ground, as they're both using the same 'CMA' point of reference).

-**Mr. and Mrs. Jones,** do you know that most agents only receive rudimentary training when it comes to creating CMAs? That's just one of many reasons why, in order to represent you at the highest possible level, we truly believed that yesterday's approach to real estate needed to change.

We have what we call a 'CPO approach' - which changes the real estate conversation in order to keep **you, the seller, in the driver's seat**. For Example - with CPO in place, when Gladys comes in with the low-ball offer, the CPO agent says:

Thank you very much for the offer, Gladys - please help me understand why it's such a low-ball offer, though?'

Gladys responds:
I did my CMA.

In this case, instead of replying with 'I did my CMA too,' the CPO agent says:

*Oh gosh, I'm so sorry. I must have forgotten to attach the **Appraisal** to the MLS. Let me send that to you. (We haven't forgotten to attach it; we are just saving face for Gladys)!*

*-Mr. and Mrs. Jones, the **Appraisal obviously trumps the CMA**. Appraisers receive extensive training, are licensed to focus on real estate value, and spend over 6 hours appraising each property.*

Now, Gladys is happy to sit down with the buyers and say, 'Great news - you have an Appraisal to look at on the home, the listing agent forgot to attach it to the MLS.'

Now we need to deal with the issues that will come up during an inspection.

Mr. and Mrs. Jones, *have you heard of a Certified Pre-Owned Car? Many car companies carry out a 156-point inspection on a CPO car, which might be a $10,000 or $20,000 car. When you go out to buy a CPO car, you know exactly what's wrong with it, up-front - and any issues have been identified, and resolved. You also get a warranty - so you can drive confidently knowing that the car will not fail.*

And yet, in old-fashioned real estate, agents will place a $200,000 - $500,000 (or even a million-dollar house) on the market, with lit-erally no inspection! It makes little to no sense - and can be asking for trouble.

Sellers:
Well I know there's nothing wrong with my house; it's well main-tained - and there's literally nothing wrong with it.

CPO listing agent to sellers:

I understand. Still, in a traditional real estate transaction, the average inspection report comes back with 25 items on it. They may be nit-picky little items, such as the hinge not working on the master bedroom door, it's squeaking, or there's something not fitting quite right, here or there.

Choose things you have frequently seen on an inspection report that are the 'small' items - you are more likely to remember these!

Mr. and Mrs. Jones:

Well, there is a drip in the bathroom faucet, and the kitchen cabinets have a couple of doors that are not quite square. All small stuff.

CPO agent to sellers:

I'm sure there are just a bunch of little things. The great thing about CPO is that if there's something larger we can't see - such as flashing on the roof, or something like that - we'll find it now. We can get competitive quotes, and take our time fixing it.

Mr. and Mrs. Jones:

I'm still not sure it's worth the investment.

CPO agent to sellers:

This approach does require some work up-front, rather than when you are in the thick of things - such as when negotiating your contract. There's another important reason it's a good idea: most often, there are two people buying a house. Usually those two people are not in agreement about the house, and they have house A) and house B) in the running. Have you two ever had that experience?

Mr. Jones: *Of course! (Points) - Jane here got to choose!*

CPO agent to sellers:

It's very easy for the person who didn't get that choice to say, 'You know what honey, since I'm the 'honey-do' person - let's just move on to the next house, please?' This may not make sense, as the next home is likely to have more than 25 items, however, the objection still sometimes becomes a lever that can be used to move on.

Mrs. Jones:
That makes sense. Those sneaky husbands!

CPO Listing agent to sellers:
Let's talk about the inspection process.

When buyers put a contract on your home, one of the first things they request is an inspection. When the results come back - though you may have thought the sale was pretty much 'a done deal' - at this point, you are essentially re-negotiating the contract. Now, the buyers can accept the home 'as is,' the price can be decreased, or the buyers can make a request for repairs. The average repair request (whatever kind of home) typically runs between $2,000 - $2,500.

Sellers:
Surely there's a list of repairs, and the agent representing the buyer gets quotes from all the different sources to fix them? And I know most of them are nit-picky little items, as you mentioned before?

CPO AllStarCertified agent to sellers:
I frequently check in with agents as to why that estimate always seems to come in around the same amount. The answer I often hear is, 'because we know it's pretty much what the market will bear!' So agents representing buyers often just come up with this 'average' figure, and present it.
-(Really).

However a pre-inspection, which we can do in the next week, takes that 'off the table.' It also affords you some time, to either choose to fix things up-front (when you have more time, because you're not in the midst of a negotiation) or to disclose any items you don't want to fix. Another key point is this: the buyers have real confidence that you're being absolutely honest about the condition of the property.

Sellers:

I will not pay $2,000 or drop my price - my home is worth a lot!

CPO AllStarCertified agent to sellers:

I agree, however, that's 'yesterday's real estate.' We do things differently. Of course it costs some money to do an up-front inspection. You have the cost of the inspection, true - however, there's a very high probability that the agent representing the buyer and their clients are going to ask for $2,000 - $2,500 anyways. So, by spending an average of $450 for an up-front inspection **(or whatever the typical cost is in your market)** *you can actually be saving a lot of money.*

Not to mention, the buyers can pull out of the contract at the time of inspection because they get cold feet. On average, there's going to be over 25 items with issues. If there's a larger issue, you may not have time to get quotes. I want to keep YOU in the driver's seat, not the buyers.

Sellers:

I just didn't realize that things were so slanted towards the buyer. What about pricing the home?

CPO AllStarCertified agent to sellers:

Most people know that the seller often drives the price. And depending on the level of experience of the agent, and whether they are hungry to take listings - they may meet with sellers and hear, 'Oh I've got to get X dollars out of it.' So, in those cases, the seller absolutely 'prices the house.'

I'm sure you agree that you should price your home at market value - and an appraiser essentially underwrites that market value.

Sellers:

Our home is not new, and we are competing with a number of new homes in our area.

Time to provide a clear outline to your sellers:

CPO AllStarCertified agent to sellers:

That's where the trifecta of the CPO comes in: **The Appraisal, the Inspection and the Home Warranty.** *Whether you are competing with homes that are not new (which we call re-sales) or new homes, offering the* **Home Warranty** *up-front gives buyers peace of mind. Let's look at a new home for a minute.*

The builder offers a builder's warranty for a year. We can offer something similar in the Home Warranty. This Home Warranty will address most issues that arise during the first expensive year of home ownership. What's more, the buyers can choose to extend the home warranty for as long as they like. When you order the **Warranty** *up-front, the good news is that you don't pay for it until closing - and you get coverage under that warranty, free of charge* (**if your warranty company offers this**) *during the tenure of your listing - only paying call-out fees, should an issue arise.*

Now you have tied up your home listing package with a bow, by offering the **Home Warranty.** *The* **Inspection** *offers buyers a home without issues - and the* **Appraisal** *presents them with a home that has a market value determined by an appraiser. For a buyer, it's as close to buying a new home as you can get.*

Sellers:

So it sounds like we can spend about $450 on an inspection, and in many cases avoid additional stress during the negotiations... reduce the threat of buyers walking (as well as the likely repair request - or demand that we fix everything) - and we will likely get a better price, as it is underpinned by the Appraisal? Along with that, we can compete much more readily with existing and new homes through the Warranty?

Sounds like a no-brainer!

Doesn't it sound like a no-brainer *to you?*

This typical conversation simply shares the highlights of what often occurs throughout the life of a transaction. When broken down in this way - where the parties have no idea what is truly wrong with the property (which may have no warranty on it), and rely on a basic tool (CMA) to determine its value - doesn't it make the 'old-fashioned' process of listing homes sound *somewhat ridiculous?* CPO addresses each of those issues, before they cause roadblocks and derailments.

 **Featured Agent**

Mark Ramsey, Team Owner of The Ramsey Group and MAPS BOLD Coach for Keller Williams, uses the CPO approach.

"There is significant value in the CPO system, which creates multiple value propositions to the seller. It all begins with what nearly every seller wants - to maximize the amount of money they get from the sale. To do this, we must entice the buyers to see the property as *the best value* of all the options they have at the time. CPO does this in several ways.

Think of it this way: if a buyer likes two houses equally, and one of them has been inspected, repaired, appraised and offers a warranty - and the other one doesn't offer any of these features - clearly the first property limits the risks for the buyer. If they choose the non-CPO property, there is a chance they will spend money on an Appraisal and/or an inspection that will reveal a value problem with the property, which could easily cause them to choose to not complete the purchase.

Therein lies the inherent problem: they will then have spent money on a house that they will never own. With the CPO house, the chance of a major inspection issue, or an Appraisal issue is virtually gone - which creates a significant positive value to the buyer. That's important, because it moves them to make an offer on that property.

Even more amazing is that the CPO Appraisal helps the seller to negotiate a higher price. This is driven by the fact that a third-party has already helped the seller to determine a price within the current market. The negotiation on CPO properties is not about the value that any of the interested parties see; it's about an independent value.

There is another hidden value to the CPO system. That occurs when The CPO Appraisal comes in lower than expected. This can shed light for both the seller and their agent that there may be a pricing issue that they hadn't realized. Understanding this at the beginning of the sales process is critical for the seller.

With all of these value items explained to the seller at the listing appointment, it becomes obvious to them that the CPO system provides multiple benefits to them. -That is the ultimate value proposition!"

Key Benefits

Key Benefits Of The Program: *CPO Assists:*

- Buyers making an offer on a home, knowing that the sellers have done all of their due diligence up-front.

- Buyer agents, who make an offer that is more likely to become a firm contract that ends in a home sale, and know they're placing their buyers into a transaction which will generate much less stress.

- Sellers who do the work up-front, and will likely enjoy selling their home with less stress, faster, and for more money.

- Attorneys, transaction managers and other real estate providers who handle a much cleaner transaction, and can focus on more important aspects of a sale, instead.

Program 4: The Listing Storyboard - Bringing A Listing To Life - AllStar Listing Storyboard™

Sections of the Listing Storyboard

1. Walking-Tour Video

2. Agent MLS description

3. Lifestyle Interview with the sellers, including pictures of the home

4. Comments from colleagues, family and friends

The Listing Storyboard is a web page or a blog post that brings a listing to life in more powerful ways than a simple MLS listing. The video, as well as comments about the home and area (from family and friends) allows potential buyers to review the home in greater depth. It also provides

Definition

a platform for sellers' engagement, through their interview, and any future comments that they want to make, as well as giving them something to share with their friends and family to help their home appear in Internet searches. It also provides an in-depth review that agents representing the buyer can share.

1. The Walking-Tour Video

A Listing Storyboard includes a Walking-Tour Video by an agent walking around with a camera and taking a good, honest look at the house. AllStarCertified agents create a video for every house, and most of them are not expensively edited. We also at times offer high-quality professional lifestyle videos, which cost

upwards of $600 (and often into the thousands). However, we *always* provide a down-to-earth, honest, good look at the house, which we embed at the top of every Listing Storyboard!

See Walking-Tour Video Program for more in-depth instructions.

Learn More

Current Price and Status HERE - Search by price
30 Black Bear Trail, Leicester, NC 28754
MLS #3273240
Presented By All-Star Powerhouse, Asheville, NC

2. Agent MLS Description

Directly under the Walking-Tour Video comes the description. This is simply a copy of an MLS description, which is improved from the MLS text (often abbreviated due to the limited number of characters) - a limitation the Listing Storyboard *does not have*. The MLS text is enriched with the 'real estate agent blah-blah' - the 'granite and stainless steel' additions, about the home, as well as the area, if the agent has in-depth knowledge of the community or town.

About This Home
2 Bedrooms/ 2 Baths
1,557 Sq Ft
8.38 Acres

With one of the most spectacular views in Western NC, this cottage has it all - acreage, privacy, structural integrity, incredible craftsman workshop, and post card views from the jacuzzi deck! PRICED BELOW APPRAISAL, with a near perfect inspection, and offering home warranty, this full CPO home won't last long. Furnishings also priced upon request. Just a short 45 min drive from downtown Asheville, located in the picturesque suburb of Leicester - you will really love this one!! Home has 3 bedroom septic permit.

3. Lifestyle Interview

The "Seller Says" portion of the Listing Storyboard is displayed below the description. The lifestyle interview with the sellers comprises such questions as:

- Where do you love to eat?

- Where do you love to shop?

- Where do you work?

- Why did you fall in love with your home in the first place?

- What is special about your neighborhood or area you live in?

AllStarCertified agents use a form to collect the answers, which are then presented on the Listing Storyboard. (Occasionally, when a customer does not have email, the 'interview' is captured by hand at a listing appointment).

Learn More

See a live form at www.AllStarCertifiedPrograms.com

"Seller Says"

There are many things we love about living in the Asheville area, especially having access to beautiful wilderness and the amenities of city life without having to ever go too far from home. We enjoy hiking in these beautiful mountains, exploring antique shops, attending craft shows, going to Drum Circle on Friday evenings, attending a variety of concerts at the US Cellular Center and Thomas Wolfe Auditorium, long drives on the Blue Ridge Parkway, spending time on the French Broad River, hiking portions of the Appalachian Trail, exploring all the interesting small towns in the surrounding area. We really like that everyone seems to have a place here no matter where they are from.

We enjoy eating out, and one of our favorite spots that is close to home is the Spring Creek Café, which is just 15 minutes away on the other side of Doggett Mountain. We also like Papa's Pizza on Leicester Highway, Sonic drive-in on Leicester Highway on Sunday evenings for a killer cheeseburger and a milkshake, Asian Wok Chinese restaurant on Leicester Highway for freshly cooked take-out or eat-in, La Carreta Mexican Restaurant on Merrimon Avenue in North Asheville, Chipotle in Asheville, Farmburger, Carraba's, Longhorne Steakhouse. We enjoy ice cream cones from Kilwin's in downtown Asheville.

We were initially drawn to what we thought was a good view, but this is truly a very special place. The house faces east, so we are greeted most mornings by a beautiful sunrise. Some mornings we are above the clouds and the mountaintops across the valley rise above the clouds and look like islands in an ocean. We also see the moon rise in the evenings, and when it is full it creates quite a show. During stormy weather, we enjoy watching the storms roll across the valley. We like lying in the hammock at

Example of form used to collect information from the sellers

Things you love about your town

START YOUR ANSWER WITH The things I love about town name are.....

Long answer text

Tell us something about your neighborhood

START YOUR ANSWER WITH, Our neighborhood is great for ....Porch parties, friendly, charity etc

Long answer text

Where do you love to eat *

START YOUR ANSWER WITH SOMETHING LIKE we love to eat at the following restaurants:

Long answer text

Grocery stores and other conveniences? *

START YOUR ANSWER WITH SOMETHING LIKE Grocery stores are plentiful and.....

Long answer text

What were you drawn to when you bought the property *

START YOUR ANSWER WITH SOMETHING LIKE when we bought the property we were drawn to ....

4. Example of comments on a Listing Storyboard

Below the Lifestyle interview, there's an opportunity for anyone to comment on the Listing Storyboard. This is wonderful for SEO (Search Engine Optimization), as each comment acts like a 'wave' to Google, saying, "look at me, I'm new!"

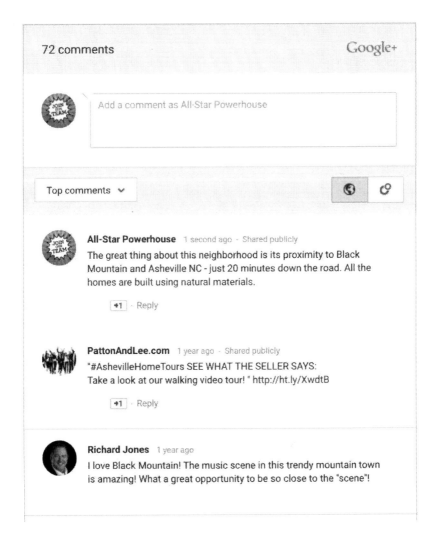

Why We Use The Listing Storyboard

As every experienced agent knows, folks move around a lot these days. Many potential buyer clients live elsewhere. When searching for a home, most buyers begin their search online, and are seduced by offers from multiple agents, as well as aggregation sites that sell 'leads' back to agents. At this point in their search, many potential buyers *only communicate online*, especially once they've surfed different sites, and have been flooded with responses from agents. When communicating with those buyers, agents have two options:

1. Send an MLS sheet (which all the other agents are sending),

2. Send a Listing Storyboard to them - which will include a Walking-Tour Video (with property information) and an interview with the seller. The seller adds interesting details, like: "Joe's WoodFire Pizza is the best pizza I've ever eaten, and the grandkids love it, too." Or, "We fell in love with this home because the entire development is really well thought-out. We're on a cul-de-sac, and the kids enjoyed growing up and safely playing together here."

The sellers share the Listing Storyboard with their family and friends, who may comment on it as well. Technically speaking, every comment acts as a 'wave' to Google, and makes it more likely to be featured higher up in searches. The Listing Storyboard really does *bring a home listing 'to life.'*

How The Listing Storyboard Came About

The Listing Storyboard is one of the first Programs I created.

I didn't like the fact that when AllStarCertified agents shared information about a house, we were sharing something from a site that was, essentially, just a regurgitation of what was already on the MLS. At that period in time, there were rotating images (sometimes called a 'virtual tour') and the same 'agent text' that we've all become used to reading when looking at real estate ads - which I refer to as: 'real estate agent blah blah.'

Because most Multiple Listing Services limit the amount of characters that can be used, they all begin to look very similar. Of course, they all contain those popular contractions one sees only in real estate - such as W/ (with) or MOM (Master On Main), DOM (Days On Market) and so on.

Still, the MLS listing only tells part of the story. In fact, due to all kinds of laws that are in place, agents are not permitted to say things that have been deemed as 'discriminatory,' nor can any descriptions be labeled as 'steering' people into certain areas.

For example, agents are not permitted to say that a homeowner could 'walk downtown' from their property. Though this phrasing is a common violation, it's been deemed an affront to the ADA (Americans with Disabilities Act). As another example, if a customer wants to know which may be considered 'the best schools' in the area, that phrase, too, is 'off limits.' Should someone want to be near a certain denominational church? *'No can do!'* Obviously, as an agent, you're not permitted to (nor would you want to) describe an area as being a 'safe neighborhood.' The point is, there are just so many things we can no longer say to potential customers that (in order to be effective at our job) other ways need to be considered!

These restrictions mean the resulting 'bland' text often explores very little about the lifestyle afforded by the potential home, which is (of course) critical towards helping buyers come to any kind of decision. The truth is, as an agent helping you purchase a home, I could likely find you one that is a good match in at least *six different places!* So of course, I'll need you to a) figure out what you want from your lifestyle, and b) think about what's really important to you. Do you go to the post office a lot? Do you need a grocery store? Do you like to buy fresh every day, or do you do a weekly shop?

So how do we figure out the lifestyle afforded by the property? For many buyers, it's as important (if not more important) than the house itself. Upon looking at a home listing, they don't get to see the neighborhood. They don't even get to see the road *outside the home.* They certainly don't get to understand what restaurants are around, or much of anything else. At least, that's the case with *old-fashioned real estate;* buyers are left to do much of the research on their own!

Better Optics

Great agents representing the buyers will get around this by *visiting a home* (when requested to do so by an interested buyer). They often make a video to send to the buyer - or use Skype, or FaceTime, or some other method - to better illustrate what they're *really getting into.* Yet imagine if that video already existed, and was part of a Listing Storyboard being shared with potential buyers.

Of course, this is something anyone can do. Complete your own Walking-Tour Video around the house, and put it out on social media channels. Put it on Facebook, YouTube, Twitter, Pinterest and all of the other social media channels on a regular basis.

Think about it from a buyer's perspective. The difference between looking at a traditional MLS sheet and a Listing Storyboard is that, with moving images, they are experiencing *actually walking around the house.* In this manner, *any buyer can* get a more vivid, detailed representation of the home they are interested in, *from their own sofa.* It's like having "boots on the ground!"

Sellers are also giving the potential buyer a more in-depth look at their home, from the outset. This resolves situations where, after their home has shown, sellers were perplexed by negative feedback, mentioning things which should've been obvious *before the showing was booked.* For example, when a home is priced to take into account a 'dated kitchen,' it can be frustrating when the feedback reads: "kitchen needs updating."

If a potential buyer reviews a Listing Storyboard, and a modern kitchen is a deal-breaker - *they simply won't visit the home.* Conversely, why would a seller want folks hell-bent on having a modern kitchen traipsing around their home, which features a 'kitchen needing updating?' In this case, videos work better *both ways.*

Once the seller's Interview is in place, which can be cut and pasted from the Google form, each pertinent location is hyper-linked to an appropriate Facebook Page. For example, when a seller Says "I love the restaurant *Que Sera in Black Mountain,*" the mention of the restaurant is hyper-linked to the Que Sera Facebook Page - and the interested buyer perusing the Listing Storyboard can then go and check out the restaurant on social media.

Putting The Listing Storyboard To Work

Once the Listing Storyboard is placed on a blog or website, copy the URL link (the www.address from the top white box)

www.ashevillehomestv.com/2011/07/check-out-this-lovely-home-at-6.html

Ptost it on the restaurant's (or other mentioned parties') Facebook (or other) social media page. Post a comment such as "Our sellers gave you a shout out as one of their favorite restaurants - please return the favor on their home selling page at (insert link)." Businesses serving consumers love the shout out, and will often return the favor.

If you have a real estate team, have your team members comment on the blog or web page posting.

Share your finished Listing Storyboard with your sellers, and request that they share it on their social media platforms. Provide them with a suggestion for an email, so they can amend to their liking. For example:

Subject: Please help us to sell our home

Dear friends and family,

As you may know, we are selling our home. Many of you have enjoyed our home along with us, and our agent mentioned that you can help us in our efforts to get it sold, and move on to be with the grandkids in Arizona. Please, simply click the link to our Listing Storyboard, which I have posted below, and make a positive comment at the bottom. Each time you make a comment, it's like a 'wave to google,' showing interest in that site, which apparently helps us in the 'search rankings.' In other words, it helps us sell our home!

www.OurAmazingHomeCanBeYours.com

Thank you; we look forward to sharing our new home with you, when we get this one sold! (as long as you click on the link :-)

Warmly, Bob and Janice

How Our Listing Storyboard Program Appears Online And In Print

See examples of the Listing on our Blogger platform at www. AshevilleHomesTV.com, and on our AllStarPowerhouse.com website by clicking on Listing Storyboards. Our Listing Storyboard allows you to engage with your own listing, and share why you fell in love with the home; where you love to eat, shop, and everything else about the city and neighborhood that you live in.

Imagine being able to share the property listing with family and friends, and the ability for them to interact with the Listing Storyboard. The Walking-Tour Video that we include is the icing on the cake - such a great way to bring your home listing to life!

The Listing Storyboard Will Allow Your Home To Compete

Most people search for their home online. They have been comparing homes using postage-stamp pictures and agent blurb which don't always help the buyer zero in on their favorite home choices.

Once a home buyer finds an interesting Listing Storyboard, they watch the video, read the story and make a comment. This provides some 'Google juice' that causes the home to move up in search lists!

Key Benefits

Key Benefits Of The Program: *AllStar Listing Storyboard Assists:*

- Buyers, who can get a clearer picture of the home, as well as the lifestyle it affords.

- Buyer agents, who can share that clearer picture with their buyers wherever they are located, before both parties spend time looking at homes.

- Sellers who share their experiences and lifestyle, and reach buyers directly through their story.

- Listing agents who have a tool to market their listings in a more comprehensive and 'personal' way.

Program 5: Walking-Tour Videos - AllStar Walking Tour™

Definition

What Is A Walking-Tour Video?

These days, buyers and the sellers alike need more support than an MLS property-details sheet and a door-opening service can provide. As very often the buyer is out of state - or too busy to stop and view the home personally. AllStarCertified agents representing the buyers set-up Walking-Tour Videos of properties their buyers are considering. It can become critical to see a property as soon as possible, especially if buyers are searching in a particularly popular area, or price point!

AllStarCertified Listing agents prepare a Walking-Tour Video each time they list a home. This is accomplished while interviewing the sellers about where they love to eat and shop, why they fell in love with their home, and more. Hyper-links are created to the restaurants and other places mentioned, so that the prospective buyers can get a more rounded view of the lifestyle afforded by the property.

Why We Use The Walking-Tour Video

In today's real estate, 95% of home buyers search online for a home before contacting an agent. Then they call an agent saying, "I want to see this list of houses." They are basing their choices on information they see on the MLS, or one of many websites which use the information from our MLS systems. This information is made up of three main things:

1. Photographs. These range from one photo of a dark exterior cell phone picture - to professionally taken pictures.

2. Agent description of the home. How good this is depends on how well the agent can write, as well as their experience.

3. Description of the features of the home, as well as legal information.

Viewing an MLS listing is a good start to get all of the basic information. The next step is to actually see the home - to walk in and get a 'feel' for how the rooms flow, including what surrounds the home.

In many areas of the country, buyers aren't always local - which can be frustrating on many fronts. They must often either wait, or plan way ahead just for the opportunity to make a 2-day trip to view a property. Sadly, when the time arrives for them to personally see and experience the home they were so excited about, it could easily be under contract with *another buyer*. This happens more than some might think. Seeing the home via a Walking-Tour Video resolves this potential dilemma, and others.

How The Walking-Tour Video Is Made

The Walking-Tour Video can be created in many ways.

DIY / Camera Tips

For the DIY (do it yourself) version, simple high-resolution cameras can be purchased for about $400 (on the low end). I'm often asked if a cell phone can be used; it is possible, however, the lighting quality (especially inside the home) will likely range from average to poor.

1. For agents who are just starting out (or who are on a limited budget) checking E-bay and local Pawn shops could bear fruit - though having a warranty may not be a possibility in those cases.

2. Look for a video camera that records High-Definition (HD) video, and supports a wide-angle view (or a camera that can take a wide-angle lens adapter).

3. An important feature to look for is "Image Stabilization"(see hand icon). This will help keep your shots steady (or steadier, at least) when walking, etc.

4. You will want a new battery - and having an extra battery is very wise.

5. Familiarize yourself with the camera, how to charge the batteries, etc., using either the camera's manual, or by entering the make and model into a 'YouTube' search, and finding the manufacturer's tutorial video.

6. Charge your batteries, turn your camera onto "Full Auto Mode" (if you're a beginner) and begin practice - simply by walking through

your own home, and describing the rooms (yes, you will be narrating)! Rest assured, you'll learn a lot watching your video playbacks - and will become less nervous with each successive walk-through!

Practice Makes Perfect!

I sometimes see home videos which have edited out the hallways and stairs. Personally, I would leave those in. It's called a 'Walking-Tour Video' for a reason; its purpose is merely to provide potential clients with a walking tour of the house. Be advised: cutting shots out of these simple tour videos (just because lighting became a bit darker here or there) can turn a 'small video project' into a much bigger one - and the end result can actually look less natural.

A cardinal rule in carpentry is "Measure Twice, Cut Once," and videos are no different. For best results, *plan your walk-through*. Then, turn on all the house lights and power-up your camera. Switch it to "Full Auto Mode," if you're an absolute beginner. Make sure your Zoom is in 'Wide' mode. Try a run (walk) - through first, practicing how best to hold the camera while looking at the screen, and walking. Then do the same thing again, while in "Record" mode. *Be careful when learning to walk and shoot!* Take your shoes off to avoid the clip-clop in the background! Have the sellers address any squeaky hinges on doors - especially the screen doors. Creaks are helpful in horror films, but not in Walking-Tour Videos!

To review, switch the camera setting to "Playback" mode. Hit "Play," and review your work. Note: in the beginning, most videos seem a little rough - but don't fret, because *All Videos Improve with Practice*.

A good, honest Walking-Tour Video is a wonderful thing. Be sure to talk about the lifestyle that is afforded by the house. Start outside, in the road - show the sidewalks, tree-lined streets, the walkway to the home, and all around the home, as well as the inside. This gives a much better overall 'feel' for where the home is located, and how it's set-up.

There is no need to be nervous about your voice being on the camera. All you're really doing is acting as an agent, representing the buyer, and walking around, showing someone the house… you just happen to be video recording it. You can stay behind the camera, as well - you don't need to be in front of it. Having a 'bad hair day?' -No problem; your hair doesn't need to be recorded, either. *We've all been there!*

For example, if I were filming a Walking-Tour Video, I might say:

Script

"Here we are at the fireplace in the great room. Imagine yourself sitting in this home, sipping hot chocolate during the cool winter months. Imagine the holidays here, with all your family and friends, and the cooking and conversation can be here - in the open-kitchen area. You also have this beautiful, open bar where everybody can sit, and still partake in the holiday festivities - without having to stay in your kitchen."

This way you're really 'bringing the property to life,' by walking around, and pointing out special features (and lifestyle) that one wouldn't necessarily notice, or consider from just an MLS sheet.

A common question is how to produce a Walking-Tour Video for a more challenging home. Find the positive sides of the property. For example, for a run-down, value-priced home that needs lots of updates, create a video that addresses other homes close by, that are well-kept and command higher prices - by way of attracting investors - or people who like to *fix up their own home their own way*, and save some money in the process.

With luxury homes, there comes a special opportunity to describe the home. AllStarCertified agents have a Program called the luxury gateway. All agents go through a series of opportunities, such as going to the local granite specialist, the local floor specialist and the local appliance specialist. The idea here is that you don't want to go into a high-end home and not know what dish-drawers are, or the differences between granite and marble, for example.

You need to have a working knowledge of basic woods. You should know what oak is, or what kind of planks are on the floor - or perhaps notice that they lay in different ways, or are randomly sized. You should know if the cabinets are hickory or cherry. The descriptions you layer into the video will be much more impressive once you've done your homework on the luxury market!

When you get the video together, you can start a YouTube account and upload it there. Once uploaded, the video can be edited on YouTube, using the basic editing options, which YouTube offers. If you're proficient at video editing on an editing software program (such as those built into a Mac, or other third-party editing programs) you may edit the video *before it is uploaded*. There are plenty of YouTube tutorials available on basic editing of videos.

Google owns YouTube, so that may help your video in the search rankings. As an agent, you can copy the URL link from the listing on your website, and put that *in the description* (on YouTube) to start building your marketing 'sticky' web. Under the YouTube title is a big box, and button titled 'description' - and you can click on it to open the description box and place a link there. This way, when viewers have stopped watching the video, they can click on the link. Experiment with 'Enhancements,' and see how you can easily stabilize the video, and correct light and color *with one click*. Searching YouTube for their 'how-to' tutorial videos is well worth your time.

What about the length of a video? It's often suggested most videos should be 3 minutes or less. You can answer this question for yourself by putting on your 'buyer's hat.' For example: if you were watching a video of a home that you were interested in, wouldn't you want it to cover every nook and cranny? Balance these issues by covering the key points of the home and neighborhood in the first minute, then elaborate until you have both the home and lifestyle well-covered.

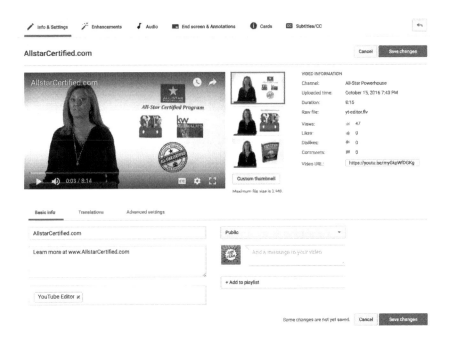

You don't even need to transcribe the video anymore - Google (essentially) does it for you! Google reaches down into the video, phishes around, and reads all the words you've spoken, greatly simplifying the Search Engine Optimization (SEO) process. That's why it's important to *mention the geography of the home, including distance from the main town, as well as lifestyle and ordinary home features.* Remember that many out-of-town buyers won't have a clue where 'Smallville' is, so providing Smallville's proximity to a better-known location will help a great deal. For example, if you live in a smaller city that is not so well known, mention the more recognized towns and airports two hours away!

You can also upload the same video directly to your Facebook page. It makes sense that a video directly uploaded to Facebook may get more views on that platform. You can also put it on a blog, or send it directly to agents and prospective buyers who have questions on the home. *Leverage all of your hard work on the video,* and put it on any channels you may have.

AllStarCertified agents place videos on Listing Storyboards, at the top. The Listing Storyboard features the Walking-Tour Video, your real estate agent information, and the interview with the sellers.

Learn More

See The Listing Storyboard Program.

When posting the videos, use hash tags (#) on social media. All the videos are then visible with one search. This will allow you to market specific topics or areas. For example: Testimonials: #AllStarVIP, Town: #AshevilleForSale

This will allow you to tag videos and market them to the appropriate audiences. For those of you new to tags try clicking on any you see on social media platforms, and you'll see that once you click on a tag, all posts with that tag will be visible. Once you have them visible (if yours is unique) you can copy the URL and share that with anyone else interested in that topic.

Note: If you think social media is 'for kids,' consider that according to Pew Research Center, a majority of U.S. adults get news on social media. Much of this news is tracked through hash tags - a way to group news, or any topic, especially on Twitter. In Pew Research Center's 2014 reports, Facebook is the most commonly used platform for news, with about two-thirds of U.S. adults using the site. YouTube ranks next, with about half of the population using the site with Twitter reaching 16%. LinkedIn is also an important player, especially in business and recruiting circles. There are a number of emerging platforms that are fast becoming popular, such as Periscope. These numbers can change as rapidly as the real estate market, so do your research!

> "YOU ARE DOING A REAL DISSERVICE TO YOUR SELLER UNLESS YOU ARE DOING A WALKING-TOUR VIDEO OF SOME TYPE ON EVERY HOME YOU LIST"
>
> ROWENA PATTON

For luxury homes (or communities) you can always have a high-end video produced. For the top of the line, you'll likely pay between $800 - $3,000 - and more at the upper end, if you're talking about 'lifestyle videos,' where you bring a 'model family' in, etc. Having a fabulous, awesome video that you paid money for is fantastic - and you'll always have that to keep.

At the other end of the cost scale, a Walking-Tour Video that you've created - which provides an honest look at the house - is serving its purpose! It's allowing a potential buyer the option to preview a property while they are working, or living in a different location. I've been quoted on stage, in my teachings and coaching as saying that as an agent, unless you are doing a Walking-Tour Video of some type *on every home you list,* you're truly doing a disservice to your seller.

 **Featured Agent**

Pedro Casanova uses the Listing Storyboard in the Miami Market.

"We use the Listing Storyboard to bring a personal aspect to our marketing with the "seller Says" section, and also share and invite all restaurants and stores which the sellers mention to visit, comment, and share the Listing Storyboard - which creates additional exposure for our seller's listing."

Pedro's Listing Storyboard At Work

Pedro Casanova
our seller loves your restaurant and mentioned it in
his properties listing storyboard. check out what he
said about your restaurant - http://www.... See More

14495 SW 173 ST 33177 - Listing Stor...
allstarsmiami.com
Very nice 3 bedroom 2 bath single famil...

Monday at 3:14 PM · Like · 🖒 1 · Reply

sushi maki
Awesome. Thanks for sharing

2 minutes ago · Like · Reply

What Is A Memories Video?

Definition

AllStar Memories Video™

The Memories Video captures sellers' *memories of the home,* which they can keep for posterity, and share with their family and friends.

How The Memories Video Program Came About

The Memories Video Program emerged years ago, after attending a listing appointment, while training someone. The sellers were an older couple, and the gentleman was in a wheelchair. He was very quiet. They needed to move into something that they could take care of more easily.

I said to his wife, "I can tell that you are really not that comfortable with selling your home.* Will you tell me more about that?" She said, "You know we built this house. Our kids grew up here. My daughter got married here. She walked down those stairs in her wedding dress." I said, "Well it sounds to me like you are really attached more to the memories, and perhaps not so much to 'the bricks and mortar' - is that right?" She said, "Absolutely." I said, "We'll make *a memories video* for you!"

95

That's how the memories video was launched.

If a seller is having second thoughts about selling their home, consider checking in with them using the following questions:

- Is it too much for you to afford?

- If interest rates have lowered, perhaps you can refinance?

- Can you benefit from my list of contacts to support your businesses?

I've helped sellers before who were struggling with their businesses. The husband was in construction, and I was able to help him market his construction business through my real estate contacts. His wife was running a sales organization, where she was selling things online. I was able to help her better market her online business, and actually keep the home, rather than sell it - which made them both happier, in the end.

Ask clients to really think carefully about the reasons they are selling their home - or not selling their home, for that matter - and to delve deep on that, because it's a very important decision.

How The Memories Video Is Produced

The Memories Video is produced in much the same way as the Walking-Tour Video. We walk around the house, just as with the Walking-Tour Video, and capture the memories of the family, and perhaps even some of their friends. A seller can share it with family, and friends. They'll always have the memory of their time in that home, and now have a great way to share the memories! It can be transferred to a DVD, or shared electronically. Home is a place of safety and security. It's important in life. Why not capture the memories - especially if it's the only thing holding someone back from selling!

Key Benefits

Key Benefits Of The Program: *AllStar Memories Video Assists:*

- Sellers, who can use this tool to capture their memories, and share with family and friends.

- Listing agents, who have a tool to help sellers feel more comfortable about selling their home, and taking their memories with them.

Program 6: COMING SOON - AllStar Coming Soon™

Definition

What Is A Coming Soon Program?

The Coming Soon Program is a platform designed to market a home *before* it appears on the MLS. It's utilized once the listing agreement is signed, often while the seller is doing last-minute preparations.

The Coming Soon Program gives potential buyers the advantage of knowing what homes will be on the market soon - in some cases even weeks before they are listed. After all, what buyer wants to miss out on a potential home, just because it's not on the MLS yet?

The Coming Soon Program's availability differs by market, depending on whether or not it's permitted by the local MLS board. In many markets it is permitted - sometimes even as a part of the MLS system.

Three Reasons Why We Use The Coming Soon Program

Reason 1) buyers see upcoming homes; sellers get 'breathing space,' to prepare to list

The Coming Soon Program is one of my favorites, especially in a market where there aren't many homes for sale (known as 'Limited Inventory'). Especially great for letting out-of-town buyers know what will be coming available, the Coming Soon Program also allows buyers and agents to register any interest in the properties - people who will be contacted *the moment the home appears on the MLS.*

Sellers love the Coming Soon Program because it provides them with some breathing space, and the time needed to get their home ready. The Program helps agents 'create urgency' for a sale.

Reason 2) Acquire the Listing at the first meeting

As an agent, it's critical to share your Unique Value Proposition at your first listing meeting with your seller.

After meeting with a listing agent interviewing to sell their home, sellers often discuss their 'upcoming sale' with almost everyone they bump into. Most of those people will have strong opinions about who the agent should be - a friend, or someone they are related to - creating what can feel like an 'obligation' for the seller to use that proposed agent. Likewise, neighbors might also begin to notice agents coming and going, to interview, and call the seller with their 'proposed agent of choice,' i.e., Uncle Joe, Aunt Gladys, Larry's best friend, the new agent next door, etc. These are clear examples of why it's helpful to *present the early advantage* of the Coming Soon Program to the seller, and what makes the Coming Soon Program a Unique Value Proposition.

Sometimes listing agents leave a first meeting with a 'potential seller' because the seller is not quite ready to place it on the MLS yet - leaving them both in a holding pattern - as *nothing has been signed.* With a Coming Soon Program in place, the required listing documents *can be* signed at the first meeting, along with the Coming Soon documentation. Then, full preparation to list the home can begin.

When AllStarCertified agents meet with sellers who aren't quite ready to list their house via MLS yet - perhaps they are prepping the house, to get it ready - the agent identifies the many advantages of the Coming Soon Program. Most sellers see the value. After getting the listing paperwork signed, agents take basic pictures of the property, write down key details and place them on the Coming Soon Program.

In her early days as an agent in Denver CO, Dianna Kokoszka, an acclaimed developer of training and coaching programs for Keller Williams, sold more than 4,000 homes. She is now the CEO of MAPS, Keller Williams' Coaching and Training Division. Dianna stresses the importance of getting the listing signed at the first meeting, including offering to call the other agents that the seller has organized to meet with, to save them the uncomfortable phone call!

Reason 3) More Time To Prepare The Home

With the listing signed, the agent then goes to work helping the sellers prepare for the sale, establishing the property as a Certified Pre-Owned home and preparing the Listing Storyboard, as well as other preparation such as staging.

Find out how to put a basic Coming Soon Program in place for free, at the end of this Program section.

 **Featured Agent**

Marti Hampton is in the top 1% of agents at Re/Max, based in Raleigh, NC. At the upper end of the 'Coming Soon Program scale' is ComingSoon.Homes, a program that Marti developed. Marti was so passionate about 'Coming Soon' that she hired a development group to build

ComingSoonHomes.com (a fee-based site) available to one agent per market, in any Franchise or Independent brokerage.

Marti Hampton's Coming Soon Program

Marti explains her Coming Soon Program over the following pages.

The Internet has brought many changes to the real estate industry in the last 20-plus years. Home buyers face a content overload that just keeps on coming; new real estate sites, new ways to get discounts, and new models to work with agents. The curious thing is that most real estate sites benefit the home buyer, and do very little beyond 'exposure' for the home seller.

About 10 years ago, I began promoting the homes my agents listed as 'coming soon listings.' We would put the sign up, do all the listing paperwork, and then usually advise the homeowner to inspect and repair, de-clutter, add professional photography, and stage the property before showings began. We began to see the benefits to our home sellers in both strong and weak seller markets.

In 2014, everything changed! We developed our local Coming Soon site, and linked it to a national web site called www.ComingSoonHomes.com, used in many markets around the U.S. The focus of this site is to showcase the listings we are preparing for market next week, next month and even longer, in some instances. The site is designed to intrigue the buyer, and make their local agent the 'hero' by knowing about homes that will be listed in the future. The idea of 'coming soon' signs is not new; in most markets (where permitted by local real estate boards) agents use that sign at the listed property address. The sign encourages buyers to call before the home is listed, helping the seller get early interest, and helping the agents garnish buyers as 'leads' who may not even be a 'fit' for that particular home.

That's where the old approach differs from ours, at ComingSoonHomes. com. Let's explore how it works, first from the perspective of market conditions.

1. In a strong buyer's market, buyers have the opportunity to view hundreds of homes. The Coming Soon program gives buyers more time to peruse a home.

2. In a sellers' market, agents put a home on the market - the home sells quickly, and everyone thinks they've got the best deal. However,

> "FILL THE ROOM WITH EVERY POSSIBLE BUYER AND EVERY AGENT THAT HAS A BUYER. THAT IS "JUST THE FACT, JACK!"
>
> MARTI HAMPTON

when a home sells at this speed, it can often mean that not all interested parties have viewed the property, *or even knew it existed!* Supply and demand is at work. There's no way you can get the best price and terms the market has to offer for any home seller, unless you take your job as Listing agent seriously, and 'fill the room' with every possible buyer, and every agent that has a buyer. That is 'just the fact, Jack!' If you believe anything short of finding all possible buyers is doing your highest and best job for your home sellers, I respectfully disagree. When did we as agents become so dependent on just MLS and Zillow to do our job?

What A Professional Promotion On ComingSoonHomes.com Offers A Home Seller:

- Increases the number of views to the home
- Front-loads the listing with heavy activity early on, when the seller has a higher level of power in the negotiation
- Intrigues the buyer
- Builds momentum and excitement for the home
- Reduces days on the market, again giving the seller more power
- Brings more opportunity for multiple offers, and therefore higher sales prices, as multiple bids tend to drive prices up

- Allows more preparation time, to provide the best first impression of the home before it is listed

- Gives the seller's home more activity, driven by FirstOpen.house module on site, as the first open house can be held, the moment the home is listed

How ComingSoonHomes.com Benefits The Agent:

- Allows more time to gain prospects from your hard-won listing efforts

- Brings leads to the Listing agent on their own listings (what a concept)!

- Provides a count of the buyers watching each home. This gives 'fear of missing out' motivation to other buyers and agents

- Features a 'countdown clock' to Opening Day

- Requires that buyers visiting the 'not yet listed' site provide accurate contact information

- Gives potential for multiple buyer prospects by using FirstOpen. House promotion

How ComingSoonHomes.com Benefits Home Buyers:

- Decreases wasted drive-by time (to homes found online) only to find SOLD sign already installed

- Provides advanced knowledge of properties so buyers can be among the first in line

- Gives the inside scoop on homes before they're listed

Here's the bottom line:

- What do we owe homeowners that often list their most valuable asset with us? In our business, just about everything!

ComingSoonHomes.com is a business strategy for a real estate team leader (or office-owner) to utilize when on-boarding new listings. It gives the agent a Unique Value Proposition that cannot be copied or equaled by their competition. ComingSoonHomes.com is exclusive to one agent in each market, and is linked to a national web presence. This site benefits a top producer or top office that intends to dominate their local market in listings taken and listings sold.

One of my favorite quotes by renowned marketing guru Gary Vaynerchuk is:

"You have to understand your own personal DNA. Don't do things because I do them, or Steve Jobs or Mark Cuban tried it. You need to know your personal brand *and stay true to it.*"

Marti Hampton, Re/Max top 1%

Putting A Basic Coming Soon Program In Place - For Free

If you want to get started with a simple Coming Soon Program, you can create one for free. For a bare-bones example of this, check the site at www. ComingSoon.House. The image below gives you a snapshot of what it looks like.

Agents will add images of the property to a simple 'Google Doc' with a few other details, and include a link for buyers and agents to register their interest. Agents also find it easy to add data, especially those familiar with Google Docs. The Google Doc with the data is then published - also a simple process - as follows:

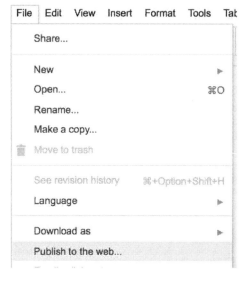

1. *First create a document in Google Docs*

2. *Click on FILE/publish to the web*

To keep it very simple, purchase a domain, and then attach it to the Google Doc link. Our basic Google doc is at ComingSoon. House. All new entries to the document become live, almost immediately.

Once the home is listed, hold an Open House the same day, and invite everyone who registered his or her interest.

Brittany Purcell, at Brittany Purcell & Associates, in Athens, GA, has a unique take on 'Coming Soon.'

"We began a 'sneak peak' system for all of our listings where the seller allows us to market the home for 48 hours before it hits the MLS. We put a cherry on top, by holding the open house that weekend, and *not permitting any showings* until the open

house. This allows us to do what no other agent has the guts to do - and as a result, we create momentum at the beginning of the listing period. In most cases, it earns our sellers full-price contracts within 7 days of listing their house. In a market where the average days on market is 92 days, I'd say *that's a win for our clients."*

 **Featured Agent**

Byeloth Hermanson is a top agent in Vancouver, WA who built-out his Coming Soon program with consistently great results.

"The Coming Soon program has been a game changer for my business. After coaching through MAPS with Rowena Patton, I grew my 'Coming Soon' offer to benefit all of my sellers - and they see the benefit, big time! The latest example is a home I recently listed using the 10-day 'coming soon' process.

After posting the 'Coming Soon' pictures and offer on various social platforms, three agents were interested in showing the home. On the day of listing, those agents showed the home, and we received *an offer over list price,* providing the sellers with time to stay in the home, after closing. Of course, the sellers were delighted! This is just one typical example of how the Coming Soon program works on my team."

 **Featured Agent**

Chris Heller is a top agent in San Diego, CA and his team utilizes the Coming Soon platform to 'double-end' more transactions.

"As inventory became more scarce, we knew we needed to adapt our business in order to remain competitive. By utilizing the Coming Soon campaign, we accomplish two goals:

1) The way we create demand for our listings is similar to the approach that big technology companies utilize to roll out a new product. By slowly releasing new information that leads up to the listing date, we generate enough 'buzz' to command more offers in a shorter amount of time.

2) We provide a competitive edge to the buyer agents on our team. Each of our buyer agents informs their clients of our team's extensive off-market inventory. In addition, they quickly pick up more clients by enticing them with our 'secret' inventory."

Chris Heller 'the home seller' has sold over 4,500 homes to date.

Key Benefits

Key Benefits Of The Program: *AllStar Coming Soon Program Assists:*

- Sellers who can get their home 'out there' in the shortest possible time.

- Listing agents, who have a way to create momentum before the listing hits the market.

- Buyers who get to see 'hidden' inventory in order to not miss out on what might be coming in the next few days or weeks.

- Buyer agents, who are showing their buyers that hidden inventory, without having to call around to agents to find out what is coming soon.

Program 7: Radio And Education Programs For Sellers And Buyers

Radio has changed our business at AllStarPowerhouse. From its humble beginnings in 2011, the show is now a robust, weekly broadcast which features planned topics each week, as well as guests who specialize in the many real estate driven topics we cover. Many years of using the show to broadcast our experience in real estate has underpinned our real estate expertise, as well as our unique approach. It's been a great way to bring credibility to our brand, as well as increasing the number of those who recognize our brand.

A large proportion of our business can now be tracked to our radio show. Often, when team members get phone calls at the office, the callers have heard the show. At its core, RealEstateNewsRadio.com is an entertainment show that happens to focus on real estate. The RealEstateNewsRadio.com show airs at 10am, live every Saturday, and can be heard via radio, a computer link, or by using the Clear Channel app found at Iheartmedia.com.

Although our show is broadcast live from Asheville, NC, we have AllStar Certified agents and top real estate agents throughout the US waiting to help buyers and sellers. Most people listen through the IHeartRadio app on their phone, therefore geography is no longer an issue in terms of reaching listeners! Listeners call in from around the country, and sometimes even internationally.

Who Comes On The Show

Each week, I take turns with other team members hosting the show. We invite various guests, covering various issues, including:

- Worldwide agents in the AllStarCertified.com network call-ins, and our loyal listeners get to hear real-world stories from diverse real estate markets.

- Team members join the group, sharing their experiences. They promote their hosting date out on social media, sharing the experience with their family and friends.

- Lenders, appraisers, builders, inspectors and other real estate professionals.

- Real Estate book authors - for example, authors of the best-selling book "HOLD: How to Find, Buy, and Rent Houses for Wealth" Steve Chader, Jennice Doty, Jim McKissack and Linda McKissack.

- Trivia Questions, which allow listeners to engage by calling in and winning prizes.

Content On The Show

The topics to be covered are planned for every week of the year. Some seasonal show content / topics can be recycled - for example, 'Valentine's Day' (and other holidays). Some main topics we cover include:

- 7 key things to look out for in home inspections.

- How your credit affects your buying power.

- Better understanding the buying and selling process.

- How to choose an agent.

- Renting vs. Buying.

- Why inspecting your home before you list it is important.

- Why Appraising your home before you list can reap benefits.

- Showcase of listings.

- Our unique real estate programs, explaining how the programs work, and what benefit buyers and sellers will get from using them.

- …And many listeners' favorite: *Real Estate Horror stories!*

Hosts have a 'cheat sheet' which includes 'intros and outros' to the show segments. The 'cheat sheet' also includes the phone number for callers to dial in, as well as the radio show name. It works well as a reminder through-out the show (and you'd be surprised how easily you might even forget *your own phone number* while broadcasting)! Ergo - when broadcasting a live show, and dealing with callers and ad-hoc questions, etc., it's helpful to be able to glance at the details.

It also includes links, which remind us to include important offers. Of course, we drive traffic to our real estate website during the course of the show, which gives details of our various offices, as well as more details about the programs we offer.

For example:

- AllStarpowerhouse.com - place to go to see the AllStarCertified agent locations
- ComingSoon.house - homes listed as 'coming soon'
- AllStarbuyers.com - buyers listed to share with potential sellers on social media and through emails
- AllStarCertifiedPrograms.com - Programs featured

Each week, a topic script is printed, which is usually a few pages of bullet points about each issue. This is handed out to the guests before the show - which are usually a host, a team member, and another real estate professional (such as a lender, or an attorney).

These items all reside in what we call the 'radio bag' - along with personal headphones, cough drops, and a bottle of water (just in case)! There's also a 'bathroom trivia book' - in case we run out of trivia questions!

How The Show Is Promoted

Welcome to our weekly live real estate real estate show! Whether you are a brand new purchaser or a seasoned seller, we have topics for you. Broadcast live every weekend, on Saturdays - call in and get your questions answered.

www.RealEstateNewsRadio.com is the radio show's website. The site has various links to topics we are discussing on the show, such as 'featured listings,' guests, etc. The radio show is promoted on our Radio Facebook page: Facebook.com/RealEstateNewsRadio, as well as our main AllStarPowerhouse Facebook Page: Facebook.com/AllStarPowerhouse

Useful Link

We often do a 'Facebook live' version of the show, so people can tune in directly from Facebook. Shows are kept as podcasts, so that we can refer back to particular topics as necessary. They are also marketed-out through other social media channels, and emails to our prospective buyers and sellers, as well as featured in our print marketing.

What If There Is No Funding For A Show?

An agent who's just starting out may lack the financial underpinning for a radio show - and seasoned agents may not have availability on a local network. Still, with the platforms available today, such as YouTube and blog platforms, *any agent can broadcast content.*

Anyone can deliver topics in a number of ways, including:

- Podcasts

- Blogs

- Video blogs

Tyler Elstrom, of AllStarCertified is a frequent host on the radio show.

"I found specific value in being an agent on a team with a radio show. It felt like we were a part of something bigger, and connecting with the community. Each year our listening base grew, and more listeners started calling in. There were times when we'd go out to lunch together as a team, and people would recognize us just from our voices - and start asking real estate questions.

There were benefits to me during each role on the team. As a buyer's agent, if I was out showing houses with clients in the car, I would turn on the radio and we would listen (excitedly) on the way to the houses. I felt proud to be part of something so big. As a listing agent, I'd reference different radio shows in my presentations, which also brought me instant credibility. Being able to feature my clients' houses on the radio was also a great value, which set us apart.

As an Operations Manager, I rigorously tracked our sources, and their return on investment - and the radio show fees consistently had one of the strongest ROI's of our lead sources. Now in Expansion, we feature one of our AllStarCertified agents on the show each week, from cities all over the country. Every agent we've featured has been nervous at first; even the high producing agents. Broadcasting unscripted to a live audience will push your comfort zone - and will probably seem intimidating at first. Still, once you get a few shows in, it's hard to describe the confidence that comes with overcoming it all! It's also been exciting to watch others go through the same metamorphosis I did. I think it's a great tool for raising the leadership lid of anyone you are coaching."

Asheville NC's AllStarPowerhouse Team Leader, Jamie Jones is a frequent host of the radio show.

"After 5 years of producing a live radio show every Saturday morning, we decided to offer the 'opportunity to host' to different agents on the team. Now, everyone involved is no longer simply a 'field agent,' but a radio host as well! The additional research entailed with each subject covered, the organization of the show and the great guests we have on have given all of us a new platform for ongoing learning - and a way to share the 'inside real estate scoop' with listeners around the country. It's become something I love to do!"

Dan Ihara Educates Through Seminars

Dan Ihara, CEO and Founder of The Ihara Team, in Honolulu, Hawaii, is passionate about education for home buyers and sellers. He delivers his wealth of information about creative ways to use real estate through weekly seminars - and has held over 800 of these so far! Topics include:

- 1031 exchange: how to use this program to help older adults create a legacy for their heirs

- Senior Living Options: helping older adults determine their options as it relates to cost and lifestyle

- Buy and Flip: Share best practices to increase wealth and profits from real estate investments

- DE clutter: The importance of decluttering when selling your home

"Our goal is to educate and inform sellers and investors so that they appreciate our unique value proposition. Years of failing forward have helped us master this lead lever. It starts with attracting sellers and investors to a safe environment where they can find the answers to their questions. We accomplish this with engaging questions that give readers a compelling reason and desire to attend. We use newspaper advertorials that give us credibility, email invitations to our 4,000-member database, social media as well as our EAA group (Elder Advocate Association), which is our network of advocates. These trusted advisors refer us clients, as well as attendees. We also partner with banks, financial institutions, CPAs and Attorneys, as well as State, City and County agencies. This networking group that we've developed has provided 35% of our business, through referrals.

Once attendees arrive at our seminars, we have a specific system, from sign-in, to their departure (at the end of our 1-2 hour seminar)."

Matt Wagner

The President of Radio And Television Experts Agency (RATE) explains where the idea for his company originated.

"I've spent the last several decades studying the most effective strategies on radio and TV advertising, working with a variety of businesses (including dozens of the top real estate agents in the US and Canada) and personalities - both on air, and with business owners that become personalities. One of the best ways I found to 'attract' versus 'chase' new prospects has been to have existing clients invite potential ones on as guests, to radio shows I already have in place. One of those was Rowena. From her interview on the air, to our first one-on-one conversation, it was obvious that Rowena had a passion for 'progression in real estate' - she loved helping others, and (I felt) would be a natural for a talk show. Also, her unique British accent made her an even more attractive candidate for a show host. The rest is history."

Key Benefits

Key Benefits Of The Program: *AllStar Radio Program Assists:*

- Sellers who get broader promotion of their listings.

- Buyers and sellers, in gaining an education on the 'inside scoop' of real estate matters.

- Listing agents, who can share their knowledge, and listings on the show.

- Rainmakers, who broadcast their approach and knowledge to a broader audience. The radio show has ongoing benefits for their brand, as previous shows are podcast.

Program 8: Priority Seller and Buyer

AllStar Priority Seller™   AllStar Priority Buyer™

What Are The Seller And Buyer Priority Programs?

Priority Programs for the sellers and buyers are designed to get planning and paperwork in place *before* directly meeting with clients.

Definition

Priority Seller Program

I HAD NO IDEA THATAGENTS WOULD MAKE ME A PRIORITY...

These days, particularly during the first few highest-activity days on the market, preparing for a home sale is critical. Therefore, before the planned listing date, my team schedules clients for either face-to-face (or phone, if necessary) appointments with key professionals (ex, inspector, appraiser, home cleaners, handymen, etc.) to ensure that all up-front preparation runs smoothly. Here are some of the things that can be taken care of before the home is listed, and why they're important.

1. **Information about the home**: gathering information about the home (such as utility costs, number of bedrooms and bathrooms, etc.) and organizing all relevant data *before* discussing the sale can save the home sellers a lot of time. My team gathers that information from the sellers through an online form, titled *'Outperform the Market When Selling Your Home,'* which you can see at AllStarpowerhouse.com *(click on VIP sellers/buyers).

2. **Listing Storyboard:** Many sellers prefer to expedite their marketing preparation by filling out our Listing Storyboard form (See Program 4: Listing Storyboard) ahead of the Listing Appointment.

3. **Checklist of Items:** We provide a checklist where sellers can set up their listing appointment by clicking a link, and contacting our Listing Manager.

4. **CPO Preparation:** sellers may call us to start the CPO Program before they list. We provide online links that allow them to request an inspector (and appraiser) before we visit to list the home. This allows the Listing agent and the seller to hold a more intelligent conversation about what price to list the home at, etc. These exchanges take into consideration what items need to be fixed (or disclosed) and whether or not items the seller is considering remodeling will bring them more money. Many appraisers will provide an appraisal both *with* the bathroom remodel or the powder room addition, as well as *in its current condition,* so that sellers can make a more informed decision.

Priority Buyer Program

Thorough preparation *to purchase a home* is equally critical in today's market.

1. After the buyer has filled in requirements on our form *'hone in on your home search,'* viewable at AllStarPowerhouse.com - (click on VIP buyer/ seller) our agents conduct a buyer consultation to explore needs and goals. Having this information up-front helps the buyers clarify what they are looking for, and helps the buyer agent 'hone in' on their specific needs.

2. In order to expedite the time buyers need to spend in the office, after a buyer consultation (often made over the phone, for out-of-town buyers) agents send out e-forms to be completed.

3. Some buyers may choose to learn more about *a* 3-6 month long Program to help improve credit, which our Lenders coordinate, titled *Credit Boost.*

4. Many folks are surprised to learn that, with a few free and simple steps, their credit score could improve - which could place the buyer in a lower interest-rate group, and may also lower insurance costs. For this, our Lenders also offer clients a *Credit Analyzer*™ program.

5. Preview videos are provided on up to 2 homes that are chosen by the buyer, often before they get into town. Some local clients also choose this service when a 'hot' property suddenly goes on the market, and they are too busy to visit the home!

Key Benefits

Key Benefits Of The Program: *AllStar Priority Programs Assists:*

- Sellers and buyers who understand the process more clearly, and prepare up-front for long-term gains.

- Buyer and listing agents, helping people prepare before looking at homes, armed with the paperwork necessary prepared beforehand, keeping the 'fun' aspect of looking at homes separate from the necessary up-front 'work.'

- Rainmakers, with a team of agents, buyers and sellers who get their 'ducks in a row' streamlining the whole process of real estate.

Program 9: Sell For Free Buy New

AllStar Sell For Free Buy New™

What Is The Sell For Free Buying New Program?

The Sell For Free Buy New Program (SellForFreeBuyNew.com) is designed for people who a) need to sell their existing home and b) intend to build a new home with the agent's preferred builder.

Definition

The basic premise is simple:

• Seller wants to sell existing home and build a new one.

• Seller contacts an agent who operates the Program.

• Seller works with a builder who's part of the Program, i.e., on the agent's preferred builder list.

• Seller agrees to use CPO (see CPO Program) and works with the agent who lists the existing home for sale.

• Once the seller purchases (closes on) the newly-built home, the builder refunds the listing commission, usually up to a certain dollar limit, which the seller paid at closing of their previous home.

This program provides a 'win-win,' by connecting builders to purchasers of their new home product, while benefiting sellers by refunding some of the commission paid.

Example

• Existing home is priced at $300,000.

- Example of 6% listing commission: Listing agent receives 3% of the home sale price, which equals $9,000.

- Seller Purchases newly-built home from a Builder in the Program, and Builder refunds $9,000 to seller after the closing.

- Some builders set limits on the refund - often between $3,000 - $10,000 - depending on the value of the new home they're offering. Sometimes the buyers choose to use the refund for upgrades on the home, which most builders offer.

See our Program at www.SellforFreeBuyNew.com

Key Benefits

Key benefits Of The Program:
AllStar Sell For Free Buy New Program Assists:

- Sellers who wish to build a new home, and are able to reduce the cost of selling their current home.

- Listing agents, who are able to assist in a reduction of costs for their sellers.

- Builders, who gain a sales pipeline of sellers who are committed to the process.

Program 10: AllStar Land Package™

Definition

In many markets, 'bare land' won't sell as quickly as homes will. Unless working directly for a developer, we found that selling one-off land parcels can be both time consuming, and expensive. Instead of deciding 'not to list land' (as many agents do), we brainstormed, and put together a package that would market these lots in a whole different way.

This includes *working with builders* to offer a pre-construction package. This program is more for land parcels that agents tend to shy away from, such as those not as desirable (due to location) or those which require development (in order to build a property) as opposed to a 'hot, downtown parcel.'

Here's how it works:

- Property owner gets an Appraisal, and lists property 5% below Appraisal, which usually makes it more attractive than other parcels that may be available.

- Agent charges an up-front marketing fee of $299.

- If the client has a builder that already has a design for the home, the lot can be marketed as a pre-construction package. We also team with builders to offer speculative ('spec') homes for the lot.

Key Benefits

Key Benefits Of The Program: *AllStar Land Sales Packages Program Assists:*

- Sellers who have found listing agents reluctant to spend time and money listing their property.

- Listing agents, who are able to market to these sellers and offer a more complete marketing package.

- Builders, who gain a sales pipeline of potential buyers who may want to use their design for a spec, or open up a conversation with them, re: their desires for their new home building project.

Program 11: AllStar Lease Option™

Definition

Similar to one-off land parcels, many agents steer away from a lease option to purchase... and sometimes for good reason! Most often, if you can get an outright sale on your home within a 'normal' period, there's no compelling reason to consider a lease option. We're all aware that the real estate industry experiences regular cycles, usually in sync with the economy - and that when the housing market slows down, Lease Options tend to become more popular. They're fairly complex to put together, and should be han-

dled by an attorney, as buyers and sellers are committing to three transactions: a lease, an option to purchase, and a sale agreement.

A Lease Option can be a good idea when a home exists in an area where there's a buyer's market (there are more homes available than buyers), or for an existing tenant, who wants to purchase the home. Lease Options are similar to any type of 'option' - they give the Optionee the right or privilege *to do something*. In real estate terms, a Lease Option allows the Optionee the right to purchase a home at some pre-defined terms.

Benefits Of The Lease Option For sellers

Many buyers who've faced challenges in the past - for example, bankruptcy, divorce, medical problems or losing their job - will benefit from a Lease Option Program. Other buyers might be in a new job position (for less than two years) or may not have saved enough of a down payment for a home. When these types of situations occur, recent poor credit history (or no credit history) can make getting a mortgage difficult. A Lease Option can allow some breathing space to repair or correct poor credit.

How The Lease Option Works

To enter our AllStarPowerhouse Lease Option Program, buyers must put down a 9% minimum deposit on the home, 'up-front.' This amount often surprises agents, who may ask: "How can someone who has poor credit have cash in the bank?" The truth is, very often a buyer's liquid cash situation has little or no bearing on their credit score; by its very nature, it is a Credit (not Cash) score! Steps:

- Seller decides their price for the home (CPO is required - see CPO).

- A deposit is set; our Program sets it at 9% (non-refundable). The parties agree how this is divided, often in this manner: 3% to the buyer's agent, 3% to the seller's agent, and 3% to the seller. When the seller closes on the home, no commission is due.

- The Lease Option agreement is drawn up by the buyer's attorney (with the buyer paying the attorney for services). The agreement is then checked and approved by both the seller, and their attorney.

- Terms are determined, such as whether the buyers are renting for a year, two years, or some other period of time. Then, the sellers and buyers agree to a monthly amount in rent. In some cases, some of the rental amount 'paid in' may be deducted from the eventual sale price.

Lease Options must be checked with an agent's brokerage and local legislation, as well as the Real Estate Commission that governs the particular state.

Key Benefits

Key Benefits Of The Program: *AllStar Lease Option Program Assists:*

- Sellers who are in a 'buyer's market', or have a home that is less desirable than the 'competition'.

- Listing agents, who can give the Lease Option seller the same consideration as a traditional seller, knowing that the compensation is not changed.

- Buyers, who are able to purchase a home earlier than they would with a 'traditional' sale.

Program 12: AllStar Estate Planning™ Program

Definition

An estate-planning Program involves teaming up with experienced financial planners, estate attorneys, moving firms and home clearance companies to simplify the process (think 'turn-key operation'). When a family is grieving, a professional, organized approach will reduces stress - across the board.

When more than one person inherits a property, many disagreements tend to materialize (such as division of personal items, furniture, etc.). Arguments about the real estate-related choices to be made also often ensue: which agent to use, whether to stage the home, paying for deferred maintenance that must be taken care of, where to store items, if necessary.

This ranges from 'simple home clearance,' to bringing in specialists for 'hoarders' - *a more common occurrence than one might think!*

CPO (see CPO) is particularly valuable in this instance, so that once an Appraisal is in place, true market value is determined - and everyone knows what items need fixing on the home through the Inspection. A Home Warranty which covers most items in the home (while it is listed) will also be in place.

If you plan your Estate Program properly, and develop a network of attorneys (and other professionals) in your area, then you will likely be the agent of choice! As few agents will be prepared to invest the time it takes to build the network - and continually educate themselves about this field - this approach can easily become your Unique Value Proposition.

Key Benefits

Key Benefits Of The Program: *AllStar Estate Planning Program Assists:*

- Sellers who are often in a delicate phase of their life to make more informed decisions about their sale, especially when those sellers comprise a group of family members.

- Listing agents, who are able to assist their sellers move through a difficult time.

- Attorneys, who often play the role of 'cleanup person' as the sale moves towards closing when the key preparation is not done up-front.

Program 13: AllStar Divorce Real Estate Planning™ Program

Definition

People going through divorce are in the midst of disentangling their joint possessions, including homes and other assets - something made even more stressful when negotiating custody of children and pets! This territory can be very rewarding, yet treacherous for real estate agents.

The 'family house' is often the most valuable asset owned by the couple and becomes 'ground-zero' on their road to divorce. Therefore, helping a couple considering separation to 'go through the motions' of understanding the process may shed some light as to how 'big' getting a divorce may be for them. Add into these financial aspects a huge dose of emotional strain and stress, and it's no wonder why, on the 'Holmes and Rahe Stress Scale,' 'divorce' takes the #2 position. Only 'death of spouse' ranks higher!

The Agent's Role In A Divorce Consultation

Sometimes a spouse who is considering separation (and perhaps divorce) contacts a real estate agent, particularly if they have a friend in the business, to get an idea of the value of the home. Agents should proceed with great caution at this stage, and advise the person to get legal advice before moving forward. Agents with a robust Divorce Program will have a 'Divorce Directory' which will contain the names of local divorce lawyers, as well as names of other useful professionals, like therapists, attorneys, estate sale vendors, movers and mediators. The directory will comprise people who the agent develops a trusted-relationship with over time, through specializing in a Divorce Program.

When dealing with a divorcing couple, remember that you are there as a real estate agent, not an attorney. Do not attempt to provide legal advice in any fashion! To do so would not only risk your license, it would also be ethically wrong; it just isn't right thing to do. They are already in a volatile and emotionally difficult situation, and you can best help them through this rocky period by helping to connect them with the appropriate professionals.

If you choose to specialize as an agent working with divorcing couples, beware of citing statistics! To illustrate this, do some research, and you'll find plenty of information *disputing the popular notion* that *50% of marriages end in divorce!* Check out DivorceRate.org and other sites for current divorce rates, which can differ greatly depending on where you live. Not all states report divorce statistics. The group of people getting married in a particular year is not the same group providing divorce statistics for that year, and between 1960 and 1998, co-habitation (the numbers of people living together without getting married) has increased tenfold. When *these liaisons break-up,* they're not noted in divorce figures.

The Real Estate Process When Divorcing

When a divorcing couple contacts an agent, it's likely they've already been working on finding solutions through one (or both) of their divorce attorneys. Still, there are some key considerations to be aware of, many which are addressed by the CPO Program.

Whether selling to an outside party, or each other, spouses using the CPO Program benefit from third parties independently (and objectively) verifying the value of the home, and identifying any repairs needed, etc. - which neither party may be aware of. As described earlier in this book, CPO not only makes for better preparation of *any* property - in divorces, it keeps both parties on 'the same page' from the very beginning, until offers come in from buyers.

In many divorce cases, one spouse has more motivation to sell than the other. Conducting CPO first allows divorcing couples to objectively and realistically discuss the bottom-line value of the home, and what will be involved in obtaining *the best price possible.* While a clear understanding of these issues not only reduces stress from the process of (and negotiations during) *any sale,* for a couple already considering divorce, it's an *absolute requirement.* Regardless of whether or not the couple decide to sell the home to a third party or transfer ownership to one spouse, CPO provides for a licensed Appraiser to set the price - rather than an agent who may be preferred by one of the parties - and thus, likely considered 'impartial' by the other.

The addition of the Home Warranty provides some breathing room on any issues that may come up while the home is listed, and for up to 12 months following the transfer of ownership.

Read the 'traditional real estate scenario' in the CPO section, and consider how well CPO applies, once those specific types of conversations between divorcing couples *begin to materialize!*

Divorce requires both parties to examine the lifestyle they've enjoyed together. Most often, money will be tighter when it comes time to establishing two new households. Divorcing spouses are wise to hire a financial advisor, to help determine whether either spouse can afford to keep the home, should one of them desire to do so. Often, one spouse takes care of payment of bills, and the other may not realize the bills involved. It's a good idea to suggest a spreadsheet, which covers all of the bills attached to the home. Everyone needs to move forward with 'eyes wide open' through every stage of the process. For example, a written agreement on what will take place *between the listing periods* and *when ownership is transferred is* critical. Determining other important issues include:

Which party will take responsibility for:

- The structuring of the buyout of the other's interest, should one spouse sell to the other. That will require assessment by their CPA, or their Divorce Attorney. This is often done with a lump sum, or through trading another asset, or a payout over a period of time (or both) - and may affect how the home is sold.

- Which party brings money to the table, if the home has negative equity (where the mortgage is greater than the value of the home).

Decisions can be made about this up-front, using the section of the listing agreement that covers this (if applicable in that state). If it is not covered in the listing agreement, the Attorney should put an agreement in place *to avoid delays at the closing that could result in the home not selling.*

- Decisions on how and when the home is shown (ex.) - 24hr notice for showings, containment or removal of pets for showing.

- How repairs are taken care of (and how will it be handled, with quotes and preferred vendors etc.).

- Paying the mortgage, how will the couple communicate this?

- The Risk incurred on the mortgage.

- Other home-related expenses.

- Set-up costs for the new mortgage, or the sale.

- Transfer of ownership on the deed, if any.

- Capital gains tax, and mortgage interest.

Legal Aspects Of The Divorce Process

Agents should consult with local attorneys to gain a basic understanding of the divorce process in their state. When entering this arena as an agent, it's also important to understand *what stage of separation the couple is at.* There are different stages of divorce, and each can depend on the state where the couple reside and/or own the property. Each stage may trigger *a different course of action in the real estate sale,* due to a domino effect on how property is divided.

Couples may start with a *trial separation,* taking some time and space to determine if this is a marriage they wish to continue being in. A trial separation can also move slowly (or more quickly) to a 'permanent separation,' by the couple deciding that they wish to live apart, with no intention of reconciling.

Legal separation may involve changing legal status, the division of property, the creation of a legal document, outlining how the property will be divided, and more. An attorney, mediator or other professional may draw up the 'separation document' - or even the divorcing couple themselves, using an online form (though this is not recommended by most legal professionals)!

What Led Me To Develop The AllStar Divorce Real Estate Planning Program

When I started my real estate career, some of my first clients were a husband and wife in the midst of a divorce. They owned a luxury home on over one hundred acres of land, which they wanted to sell as part of their divorce agreement. At that time, I knew that, considering my level of experience (or lack thereof) I would certainly need some professional assistance. I brought in a land specialist - Cathy Dickinson - who helped me gather all relevant information required, and also acted as a co-listing agent.

There were many challenges. At 6.9 million dollars, my clients' property was the most expensive listing on the MLS. It was also somewhat remote, with few properties to compare it to, and (of course) the sellers were divorcing. Needless to say, I went through a huge learning curve! Since that time, and after stepping through some delicate conversations with divorcing clients (as well as friends) - I've learned the importance of developing a tried and true support team, and process, to assist divorcing couples.

While developing the AllStar Divorce Real Estate Planning Program, I reached out to yet another talented professional, Laurel Starks, and soon discovered that we both shared a similar experience in dealing with a divorcing couple, early in our careers.

Featured Agent

In 2006, Laurel Starks was appointed as the agent to sell a home that was a court-ordered sale, due to a divorce. The divorcing couple had a son together, and the husband had a girlfriend; it was, to say the least, an uncomfortable situation. The home was a mess, with boxes stacked around. Plumbing and various other issues were apparent. When Laura introduced herself to the husband as 'the Listing agent,' he said: *'Over my dead body!'*

"WHEN I TOLD THE HUSBAND I WAS HIS LISTING AGENT, HE SAID, 'OVER MY DEAD BODY' "

LAUREL STARKS

That experience catapulted her into researching this field, in order to serve her divorcing clients at the highest level. She now trains other agents through her *Divorce Institute*, at (DivorceRealEstateInstitute.com).

Laurel's book *"The House Matters in Divorce: Untangling the Legal, Financial and Emotional Ties Before You Sign on the Dotted Line"* is useful reading for any agent interested in specializing in this arena. She is a recognized expert in family law / real estate, and has presided over $120 million in sales volume.

Learn More

Key Benefits Of The Program: *AllStar Divorce Real Estate Planning Program Assists:*

See AllStar Estate Planning

Program 14: Referrals

Most successful agents have learned that referrals from clients (or another agent) can be the most productive and rewarding way to build their business. Referrals to the agent come in from happy clients who are confident and proud to refer the agent to their friends and family.

Learn More

There are some great books written on building your referral base, and Michael J. Maher's bestseller 'Seven Levels of Communication' is one of them. One of the many things Michael's book explores is *the layers of the referral,* which covers the importance of reaching out to the person who actually *introduced you to the person* providing the referral.

In 2014 The National Association of Realtors (NAR) published a report (2014 Profile of Home buyers and sellers) which identified that more than half of all buyers and sellers find their agent *through personal referrals.* Those are passive referrals that 'drop in an agent's lap.'

Active referrals are those that an agent seeks, through ongoing communication and a relationship with forever clients, as well as other agents. Although many buyers and sellers state that they are happy with their agent at closing, the majority do not use the same agent the next time they have a real estate need (that need often arises many years later.) This is usually due to the lack of a robust follow-up system that offers value to forever clients. Perhaps we are so focused on the immediate gratification (and hard work) that comes from working with a current buyer or seller that we neglect the long-term pipeline that forever clients represent.

Building a referral-based business takes long-term planning and work. Imagine the difference between stuffing a pipeline with thousands of expensive Internet leads - which we know convert to contracts around 2% of the time - and building a robust business based on referrals from clients. Consider the cost differences and time investment of the two approaches.

It's easy to conclude that building trust with current and previous sellers and buyers provides an ongoing pipeline of business. Striving to consistently 'do the right thing' by always 'putting the client first' may seem cliché, however, the pursuit of these goals is *always rewarded over time.* Like most businesses, real estate is not a sprint, but rather a long-distance marathon.

An important step in gaining referrals is to pay attention to your reviews. Review companies are part of a growing industry which offers to take care of your 'presence and branding' online. If you don't have the funding or time to hire a specialist right now, it's a good idea to focus on the two or three platforms most important to your business. Remember, if you build your review presence on any platform that also sells agent leads, you are also helping to build that company's presence online. If you are starting from scratch, start building your reviews on your Facebook business page.

Reviews are becoming increasingly important, as buyers and sellers can easily research agents online before getting in touch with them. Your review is an important part of your online presence, often called your 'digital handshake'. Make sure that handshake is firm and professional, not clammy and limp! Build a plan to assess your presence online, and make sure that it is visually coherent, and clearly delivers your Unique Value Proposition. You can make it as awesome as you want, however, without that UVP, it's going to look like just another glamorous profile.

The conversations we call Reviews and Referrals are directly tied to your Unique Value Proposition. If you have communicated your 'magic,' your friends and colleagues will have something to say about you that's different, and you will stand out from the crowd.

Tyler Elstrom

Tyler Elstrom began his career as a Buyer's agent, then a year later shifted to a Listing agent role, onto Operations Director and manages AllStarCertified, the AllStarPowerhouse network.

In his role as an agent, Tyler specialized in an area that many agents find difficult - working with For Sale By Owner (FSBOS) and Expired Listings.

"I heard about a real estate study conducted where they identified that a person can only have 2 real estate agents in their head at all times.

Interestingly enough, I'm fairly introverted, so - no matter how much I cared for past clients, I found calling them over and over again to follow up difficult, strictly because of the phone-time. The average person buys and sells every 7 years. No matter how wonderful you are, chances are they might forget your name over a 7-year period if someone else is more consistent than you are with communication.

I realized that I had to adapt and get a system going, or my clients were going to forget about me. The second thing I realized was that most agents are scared to follow up with FSBO and Expired leads, and by focusing my systems on these particular clients, I could make a huge impact on my business and convert clients that many people were scared of.

My approach to FSBO's and Expired listings was different than what people will typically read in other books. I threw out all my scripts, and came from complete contribution. Most people list their house for the same reasons - we call it the three "D"s of selling: Death, Divorce, and Debt. These are emotional topics, and ones that most of us have experienced ourselves - whether personally, or through a friend. If an agent walks into that situation with a sales script, is too polished, or doesn't seem human, they just aren't going to get very far.

Someone going through an emotional process is looking for a human they can connect to. I worked hard, and was able to find a likable balance between being vulnerable and professional. This turned into a huge value proposition in itself. As I was courting these clients and consistently following up, I would tell them how to sell on their own, what scripts they were going to get, and what to watch out for if they got an offer from a buyer's agent. I would pour into them each time I called.

As they'd already seen how trustworthy an agent I was, I always made it clear that I wanted to be the first person they interviewed, when they were ready - and that if they bought, or had a friend who needed an agent, that

I'd be ready to take care of them. In a sense, I was following the best advice I'd been given about real estate, and life itself: "always make a deposit, before you make a withdrawal." That was years ago, and I still have those clients contacting me monthly, with referrals from the deposit I made with them as they were selling.

The biggest point I can make is, if your goal for the day is to set an appointment, or get a listing, you're doing it all wrong. My goal everyday was to help as many people as possible. The money and business were the byproduct of doing a great job - and falling in love with every single client in my database."

Tyler Elstrom, Asheville NC

 **Featured Agent**

Christopher McNamara founded a Keller Williams MAPS coaching program that trains and coaches agents to build a stronger referral base. Agents are coached once a week, one on one, and benefit from the group's masterminds (as well as from the tools, and systems library).

"Webinars can be a "gong-show" of edutainment. It was a neat parallel for what we were sharing, because we were attempting to deliver value into crazy-busy schedules *of people attempting to deliver value;* which can soon start to feel like 'painting hummingbird wings!' So, each session's a test of how well we're really executing the multi-channel experiences of getting in touch with, and reaching people. Did the video's message land? Was the question in the Facebook group responded to? Did they follow the call-to-action in the text? When the content is good - where it just makes NEW sense, where you can HEAR the eyebrows go up on a webinar? That's when we're clicking."

Chris explains: "when you consider any business, leads and contacts seem to be the fuel to keep any engine running, and you're going to have exhaustible and renewable resources. Cost per lead, market conditions, governing rules of 3rd party Internet providers, can monkey wrench a lead source - overnight!

What's NOT as volatile is your influence, specifically on the people in every one of the 3 zillion areas in your life; helping your barista Cindy choose a condo building is just *something you do,* because you're a good person - not because "she represents the target audience in your '24-33' B2B allied resource graduation campaign" - even though she does! And the same way that **anything** you grow can happen naturally in the 'wild,' the chance to help in a relationship can also be systematized - to occur quicker, better, and at a higher volume. The hurdle we have here is we get that **salesperson vibe** going; and if this worked for one barista, I'm going to blanket the town with my 'solution' *for every barista,* even if they don't have the same question.

People aren't plants, stocks, or widgets. Yet the actions we take to stay top-of-mind, and in a positive experience can be that system; the mediums we take them in - and the order in which we take them - individually are *skill sets,* put together to form your competency *of a solid experience with each client.*"

Program 15: Providing The Highest Level Of Service For Clients

AllStarCertified agents pursue high goals of ongoing service in a number of ways. *The following list excludes activities which my team would consider 'givens;' for example, ongoing, weekly communication with the sellers, and marketing efforts such as testimonial videos and procuring reviews on websites.

Our systems include:

For buyers

- Develop a checklist of buyer's potential needs, (we call it a buyer survey) which each agent completes at the initial buyer consultation. (You can see our initial survey at AllStarPowerhouse.com, click on VIP sellers / buyers).

- Set up a property search, which accurately reflects the buyer's needs, one that automatically emails the client (instantly) when a property that matches their needs is listed on the MLS.

- Assess whether needs have changed, by maintaining frequent contact with the buyer - regardless of whether they are purchasing now, or in the future.

- Have a website which provides more than matched homes, which includes details about neighborhoods, lifestyle and employers, etc.

- Have a website which allows searches for specific needs - for example, homes with elevators, pools, or condominiums that allow pets, etc.

- Develop programs that help the buyers, such as the AllStar Love it or Leave it Program, or the Preferred buyer Program.

For sellers

- Produce a list of buyers (see an example of ours at AllStarbuyers. com) that the sellers may peruse. This list comprises buyers *who have signed an agency agreement to work with our buyer agents*. It's also shared across social media and other marketing.

- Share the *list of programs* with the seller. This includes The CPO Program, Listing Storyboard and other programs designed to solve particular problems that sellers often face. Empower the seller by engaging them in the sale, through the Listing Storyboard, etc.

- Have a website that meets buyer's needs (described above in *For buyers*).

- Set up a *Market Watch* search, (similar to the buyer search also described above, in *For buyers*) with the subject line *"SOLD! - What is selling in your zip code / neighborhood etc."* In the property search alert, the 'under contract' choice box is checked, so that the moment something sells, an alert is sent to the seller, so they can observe the market (in their 'hyper-local' area).

For buyers and sellers

- Have a *guaranteed response time*. Sellers want to know that any buyers making inquiries on their listing will be contacted within 5 minutes (or whatever the agent's standard is). Likewise, buyers want to know that they can speak with their agent when they get excited about the home they want to put an offer in on - *tonight!*

- Share the agent's organization chart - showing others available to answer questions, such as the Listing Manager and Transaction Manager, who are more likely to be available than a successful agent out in the field showing and listing homes.

- Have a 'mentor' program in place. AllStarCertified agents come into the team as 'Concierge agents', learning our systems and setting buyer and seller appointments *before* working with clients in the field. Once they have a number of contracts pending (from their appointments) they can (if they wish) move on to a 'Partner agent' role, where an experienced Lead agent tutors them through the buying and selling process. This mentorship is rewarded through sharing a percentage of the Partner agent's commission. A Partner agent becomes a Lead agent after assisting with a set number of contracts. This gives our buyers and sellers confidence that agents who've been trained at a higher level are assisting them.

- Have a coaching program in place for buyer and seller agents who do not consistently receive high scores (from clients) for giving the highest level of service, triggered by a trend of that agent not hitting a standard. Individual agents can employ a coach for this.

- Maintain a weekly leadership meeting. We do this through a weekly 'leadership lunch' where any quality issues (as well as other points) are raised, and discussed.

- Develop a system that surveys both buyers and sellers at every point of the relationship, systematically monitoring (and documenting) their level of satisfaction. Links to the survey are provided below all agent emails, as well as on e-mail 'drip' programs. At our weekly meeting, the team reviews all results, for all agents. The AllStarCertified survey includes the following questions, and can be filled in by the client (or a sales agent, over the phone).

Example

Example of the Survey used by AllStarCertified agents

All-Star Powerhouse Customer Service Survey - Asheville

We strive to offer the highest level of service available in the real estate industry. We also know there is always room for improvement and fresh ideas. Can you help?

* Required

Your initial contact with All-Star Powerhouse @ Keller Williams Professionals Realty was made through *

- Already a client
- Print Advertising
- Referral from friend
- Referral from another agent
- Weekly Radio show
- Internet Advertising
- TV
- Other:

Which factors made you choose to work with All-Star Powerhouse @ Keller Williams? *
(#1 in market, innovative programs, communication, responsiveness, assistance throughout process etc.)

Did your agent provide you with sufficient information to make a good decision? *

1 2 3 4 5

Poor ○ ○ ○ ○ ○ Fabulous!

Were you kept as informed as possible throughout the process? *

1 2 3 4 5

Poor ○ ○ ○ ○ ○ Fabulous!

How would you rate the level of your agent's communication, overall? *

In addition to our agent Service Survey, we also have a survey which checks the performance of our vendors. As transactions occur, the agents fill in the survey, and results are viewed at the weekly agent meeting. These results are openly shared with the vendors, who are often present at the meeting.

This requires work - still, it may be the most important process we incorporate to ensure that we are continually improving. All of the above checks and balances help us maintain our high standards, thus bringing more referrals from our clients.

With all this emphasis on effective real estate Programs designed to help the customer (and still make the agent stand apart), something would be missing if we didn't explore Mike Hick's 'The Promise!'

 **Featured Agent**

Mike Hicks, The Promise

Mike Hicks is an Idaho Falls-based agent who helps more than 300 families buy or sell their homes each year. He's created a 'Promise' around his business that projects the core value proposition of his organization. At first glance, his program may seem fairly straightforward. However, upon deeper investigation, one comes to understand that Mike's well developed, 'customer-service / quality-control system' drives  his entire organization, *while clearly separating them apart from the competition.* As a result, Mike Hick's 'Promise' provides a classic example of 'the win-win' - especially when Mike is showered with referrals from satisfied clients.

During a conversation with Mike, he shared his philosophy of customer value:

"We make a promise to *everyone we do business with.* We intend to create this amazing customer experience - and everything we do is focused around delivering on that promise. We know there will always be challenges in every real estate sale, or search. Our clients know that everyone in our organization is focused solely on *their wants and needs*. We get out in front, and stop the surprises early on."

Mike generously agreed to share his script for the Promise; you will find the 'script' in *italics*, and 'help notes' in (**bold, non-italic parentheses**):

(**Start with a transitional statement such as**)

Script

So, before you go, there is one other thing...do you have another minute?

OK, let's talk about 'Our Promise'.

Our group has this 'Promise', a 'Goal' to create this experience you <u>really cannot imagine being better.</u>

- *Our systems and everything we do are designed around <u>delivering on this Promise.</u>*
- *Everyone in our group is focused on <u>what you want,</u> and need.*
- *We make every effort to be out in front of everything, to <u>stop the surprises,</u> and keep it as good as it can be.*
- *Now <u>there will be challenges,</u> we know there will be, it's real estate after all, and it's people!*
- *Just know that to a person, our group is focused on creating <u>that '10+' experience,</u> if you will.*

.....<u>And That's Our Promise!</u>

Doesn't that sound great?

(**Wait for response**)

So, there <u>is</u> something that I want.

(**Smile and get some humor in at this point**).

- *Just to say it, another goal we have is that some time from right now* (**pause**) *until the day we close on your home, is...*

    o *...That you will _feel so great about what we are doing for you_, that _you will call me_.....text me.....or email me with the name of somebody that needs help in real estate.*

    o *That person might just have a general question, they might need to buy or sell a home, they might need to refinance; they may just need help with real estate in general.*

Do you think you could do that?

To be sure you understand what I'm asking, while we are working together, you will hopefully be giving my name out, which I truly, truly appreciate. Word of mouth is our lifeblood.

- *What I'm asking is that you _take the next step,_ to make sure _I have a chance to help_, in addition to giving my name out, please call.... text.....or email me their information...*

- *Because then there is a 100% chance that I'll get in touch with them.* (**Pause**)

- *Can you do that?* (**Wait for answer**)

- *OK, that will be great, _so you will call, right?_* (**Wait for answer**).

- *OK, that would be perfect!*

Now, if we get to the date of closing and we are sitting at the closing table,

- *We've signed all of the paperwork and _you haven't been in touch_ with the name of someone we can help,*

- *I'm going to assume that _our group didn't deliver on the promise_.*

- *That we _could have done better_.* (**Pause**)

- *So I'll want to talk to you about it, and find out what we <u>could have done differently</u> in order to have earned that referral. We always want to improve.*

- *Will that be OK with you?*

Well OK {name} I am going to count on it. I am going to <u>count on you being satisfied</u> - and on you <u>sending that referral</u>. **(Shake hand; touch on arm or some form of physical connection)**

Mike goes on to explain how *The Promise* permeates his organization, and how critical that is:

"My support group is a critical part of us keeping our Promise, and always delivering excellent service. For example, once a home's listed, the Listing Manager has an introductory call:"

- *Hi, and welcome to our Success Team - I will be talking to you every week. I know that Mike talked to you about our Promise.*

In other words, Mike's Listing Manager and the other members of the support team reiterate *The Promise* at every connection point. This is not an agent promise. This is an *organizational promise* - and everything Mike's team does is designed around it.

Mike gives an example of how the team keeps their Promise:

"A client was moving to our area, and driving up from San Antonio. En route (and this is during a weekend, mind you) his car's transmission blows. He calls into our office, distraught; his furniture is being delivered *as he calls in*. He's purchased a home he hasn't seen. The moving company told him that it would cost him an additional 13 thousand dollars to store his property, as he was not present to accept it at his new home. Our Office manager and support group got together; made calls and rotated schedules to make absolutely certain that *someone would be present* to get the furniture.

When our office manager called and told the client, he broke down and cried."

It's clear to our clients that our organization really cares about them."

For more information about Mike's program, contact his office at:

(208) 227 5320

Key Benefits

Key Benefits Of The Program: *AllStar Service Program Assists:*

- Agents, to connect with their database in a systematic way.

- Rainmakers, in using feedback from systematic surveys with their prospects and clients, checking in on Vendor offers and agent service, and using constructive feedback to grow their business.

- Agents with a robust pipeline of sales that come from the least expensive source of 'leads' - those people who already know and trust us through a previous experience.

Chapter 3:

About the Author: Growing Perspective

Life At Home

While planning this book, the publishers discussed adding in my early story. After first resisting, I realized that a lot of what I have experienced has led me to look at people and things differently, through a lens which founder of Keller Williams, Gary Keller calls *'my slant.'*

Like many kids who experienced a traumatic childhood, as an adult, I love to watch others succeed at high levels, and to do everything in my power to help them identify roadblocks and maneuver around them. Most of the Programs described in this book came about this way; focusing on the roadblocks miles ahead, and clearing them before they cause delay.

I grew up in a difficult home environment, and therefore spent a lot of time with my grandparents in Coventry, UK. From my earliest years, my childhood was littered with cuts, bruises, and fear - and being as quiet as a church mouse at home was a full-time survival skill. Running my *Etch-A-Sketch*™ too loudly could lead to a beating. Eventually, though, angels stepped in. My wonderful music teacher began bringing me to her home for practice, and other teachers (and friends' parents) also stepped in to help. Whenever the opportunity arose, I found myself at someone else's home.

My grandfather was a wonderful male role model in my life. He threw a lot of challenges at me; taught (or attempted to teach) me to play chess before I could read, and how to read a giant, old-fashioned logarithm book he gave me at age 6 - while I was learning the 2x table at school! He was interested in music, and would book me into clubs to compete around the country, as what we now call a 'child performer' (albeit a very shy child performer). He also took time to explain to me how things worked, and we often took machines apart, and then put them back together. Which was fun, until when (at six years old) I took apart the tiny piano he'd brought back from Austria, *to see how it worked!* (Sorry Grandad. I know you are still watching).

Sadly, my grandfather passed away when I was thirteen. Upon reflection though, the best gift he (and grandma) gave me was in helping me avoid 'generational fences,' by opening up their world to me, despite my very young age. I came to know their aging friends, and developed an early insight into 'older people's lives.' Essentially, I gained the gift of understanding that, fundamentally (and regardless of their age) people's behavior and values are really not so different, after all.

At 15, two years after my beloved grandfather's death, and dealing with my life at home, I was depressed and anorexic, and had been sinking for years. Eventually, I tried to take my own life. I failed at this (fortunately) - however, that evening I saw a fast-forward video of my life pass in front of me. Quite an experience. I woke up alarmed, thinking I was in heaven - yet remember looking around, wondering: why had God placed me in an exact replica of my poky little bedroom? Although I was relieved that it was, in fact, my poky old bedroom... the time had come *to sink or swim.*

The College Years

A few months later, when I was almost 16, there was (not surprisingly) yet another ugly incident at home, during which I finally snapped, and ran away for good. Fortunately, my boyfriend's family opened up their home to me, with whom I stayed for a year, through 'junior' college, before moving south to study at the University of Northampton. While studying marketing and graphic design, I paid for my college years going door-to-door, selling textured coating for homes (5-7pm) - bar-tending later (7-11.30pm) - and working at a home improvement center on Sundays, to pay my way. These were challenging and exciting times, from which I learned a lot about life, sales - and perseverance.

I finished college just before turning 21; around that time, my grandmother passed away, and left me their tiny two-story row house. I had lost my angels, yet retained the 'safe haven' I spent so much time learning and growing up in. Still, their old house was in need of some repair and remodeling, the undertaking of which became my first foray into real estate.

I ripped out the central staircase, all the old plaster and lathe on the walls, doors, windows - and practically every part of the home - including the outside bathroom. It took almost 6 months to replace the staircase. I went to work every day at my first 'real job', then returned to the chaos, until finally, I decided it was time to live somewhere else for a while. Still, when all was said and done, I ended up with a home I was proud of - which was re-built on a budget. My real estate journey had begun!

Work Life Begins

For the next 10 years I worked for a marketing company, which I began fresh out of college, at 'entry-level,' assisting with marketing and sales operations. It was a wonderful experience that (eventually) had me working with small businesses in practically every industry you can think of.

There were two directors - one of whom had (allegedly) committed enormous fraud, to the tune of hundreds of thousands of dollars. He was writing company checks and forging signatures to buy jewelry for his mistress. Eventually though, he was discovered - and faced either going to jail, or being fired. (He chose the latter). Before he was fired, however, I remember staying late to meet deadlines, and chatting with him about all the value I was bringing - basically asking how I could be paid more than the minimum wage I was receiving. I'll always remember his words of advice: *"Rowena, it's not about the money that you have, it's about what you do with it."* Although hindsight makes that statement ironic, there's still some truth in what he said.

Once he was fired, the remaining director, then facing a bankrupt company, said: "Rowena - do you think you could become a director?" We had 8 employees. While still only 21, I'd worked my way up in the company through driving sales activity... so I said, "Sure, yes - let's do this." That company became Cotterill and Patton.

Because of the financial mess, we were required to appear before the bank every month, to show our Profit and Loss (P&L) statements (which I actually thought was normal). I can't believe the banks stood by us - but they did. The Bank of Scotland really came through. This period taught me a great deal about running a business, and how to create winning sales strategies and marketing for companies of all sizes.

Ever since then, the recurring lesson (gift) of 'digging in' and persevering when times get tough has served me well. After all, everyone finds it easy when the going is good. However, we all learn more about people - and ourselves - through witnessing how things are handled when *life throws us curve-balls.*

As an executive at the marketing company, to support our endeavors, I launched both a public relations company and a photographic imaging company. I worked in almost every type of industry, creating marketing materials and sales strategies for all kinds of companies, e.g., IBM, a chain of sandwich stores, a London Taxi supplier, and a catalog-direct sales firm. We even worked with a chain of funeral parlors!

At that time, the European Economic Community or EEC (now called the European Community) was high on our company's agenda, as well as Europe's agenda - of course. I was determined to expand and join forces with other marketing companies in Germany and France, the idea being to more effectively market companies throughout Europe. We set up a network with companies located in Berlin and Paris. This was my first experience in 'Expansion' - a strategy Gary Keller, founder of Keller Williams, would be coaching me on, 20 years later, in the real-estate realm.

In 1996, through one of my long-term clients in the marketing company, an opportunity arose to work in the United States. My client had been working for the board of a company, Zurich Financial Services, which was among the top 3 financial-services companies in the world. Headquartered in Zurich, ZFS owned numerous American-based companies. The job position I filled was a Management Consultancy role for ZFS's board in Switzerland; it entailed assisting their leadership with the planning and marketing of programs that were to be their *development initiatives for 300 CEOs around the world*. For the next seven years, I traveled throughout the U.S. and Europe. Chairman Rolf Hüppi charged me with interviewing all of his CEOs around the world - mainly to ask them to expound upon one question: *'What's the key to your **success?***'

The objective was to find out the core competencies of his successful leaders. During these interviews, I discovered that a few key elements were in their 'humility,' and in the perseverance the leaders had throughout more adverse times. The majority of CEOs credited their successes to the amazing teams surrounding them, and to those who offered their hand to help others 'up the leadership ladder.' They all clearly understood that their success was built on supporting both individuals' and teams' successes, along the way.

During my time as a consultant, I moved around the US quite a bit, which included cities like Washington, DC, Los Angeles and Miami Beach - before settling into the Asheville, NC area in 2006. During that time, I'd also purchased and remodeled many homes and condos around the country, either renting or 'flipping' them.

In 2006, I decided I would 'take a year off' - though (of course) things didn't really pan out that way! In any event, after traveling internationally for years, I felt as though my personal life had suffered. I needed to take a breath, and slow things down - perhaps even gain some new perspective. Indeed, he perks and wonderful scenery went hand-in-hand with jet lag and stress - and often the inability to enjoy my own home for more than even a few days at a time.

After moving to NC, my 'year off' was largely consumed by a new house (read: project) that included ripping an upper floor apart, and multiple other time-killing requirements that 'new houses' often bring with them.

Also came the purchase of a 1920's four-unit building in Asheville, which was historic - but dilapidated - for the purpose of remodeling into luxury condominiums. This 'Patton-Flint House' (in Historic Montford) began with an unfortunate real estate experience, in what would be my last role solely as 'a real estate customer.'

The property featured both an underground storage tank, as well as asbestos in the basement (a particularly 'touchy' challenge for a 'historic district' property) - neither of which were disclosed during the transaction. Once these were discovered (after the purchase) the ramifications of remediation (in terms of time spent, cost and major safety issues) were extreme. The geriatric underground storage tank had deteriorated - resulting in its removal - and cost tens of thousands of dollars (as large margins needed to be dug out, to remove any contaminated soil).

I could have just ignored the issue, as it wasn't disclosed - and the 'fill pipe' had been cut down (and thus disguised). However, I soon imagined cars driving up and down the driveway over that old, buried tank, putting pressure on the surface and eventually leading to its collapse. One day, I figured, some small child could fall into the old, rusty metal container.

...And Then Came The License

After a great deal of time and energy, I got through it all... but *what a waste* of time and energy! I later learned that (unfortunately) many other agents also had 'bad' experiences, early on (as real estate 'customers') - which also eventually drove them to acquire *their own real estate license.* Likewise, while knee-deep in the remodeling of 'Patton-Flint' house, I too felt 'enough was enough' - and decided it was *time to get mine.*

Rather than being fearful about buying or selling a property, I felt that the experience should be exciting (and even fun) - as in many cases, those involved are moving into another chapter of their lives. What could be more exciting than that?

My career in Asheville real estate started in 2007, with Keller Williams Professionals. Because of my English accent, some of the locals told me that I 'spoke funny,' and that (as a result) I'd have a hard time getting into the business. They also warned that I had 'no *sphere of influence*' here, which means 'no folks you already know.' Now (ten years later) I have the top team in the Asheville NC market, and the #1 spot on the MLS for the last few years. I knew that if I could do it (with all of my encumbrances) then others could, too.

I've accomplished that by both constantly looking at real estate from the customer's perspective, and choosing to work with amazing people. As you've read, I've been *that customer,* been through those horrible real estate experiences, one too many times. So, I would ponder, what would it take to make that experience better? Because the truth was, the way we've been doing real estate in the past *just isn't working anymore.*

In 2007, the first year of my real estate career, I was the Rookie of the Year (as an individual agent) with around 40 transactions and a volume of 12m. This was the beginning of the banking crash, and as a consequence the real estate sales decline. Everyone I knew thought I was crazy for getting into real estate.

The truth is - for that first year - I agreed with them! Having come out of an international management arena, the real estate processes we used seemed absolutely antiquated to me. I couldn't understand why we were expected to do *everything* in real estate - be the salesperson, the marketer, the listing agent and the agent representing the buyer, the budget person, etc. - all very different roles. I was distraught. And then, through my experiences with Keller Williams, I learned how to build a strong team - and the importance of surrounding myself with *those who shared my vision!*

As John Doerr, Chair of Venture Capital firm, Kleiner Perkins, says so clearly, "You must ask, 'Are these the people I want to be in trouble with for the next 5, 10, 15 years of my life?' Because as you build a new business, one thing's for sure: You will *get into trouble.*"

Keller Williams has always had a robust portfolio of training programs, earning them the accolade *Top Training Organization* from 'Training Magazine' (for both 2015 and 2017). The company is also unique in its commitment to the formation of 'real estate agent Teams.' Keller Williams developed programs which not only trained agents to recruit and select *the right people*, but *how to best lead and motivate them* as well.

"YOU MUST ASK, 'ARE THESE THE PEOPLE I WANT TO BE IN TROUBLE WITH FOR THE NEXT 5, 10, 15 YEARS OF MY LIFE?' BECAUSE AS YOU BUILD A NEW BUSINESS, ONE THING'S FOR SURE: YOU WILL GET INTO TROUBLE."

JOHN DOERR

At the start of my real estate career, I attended what was then called '*Recruit, Select, Train, Lead and Motivate '(RSTLM)*' nine times. Though fascinated by a proven, thorough process to hire and lead, I didn't exactly come 'roaring out of the gate.' Like many 'mega agents' I went through a roller coaster of team-building, training and expansion 'stops and starts' ...however, in almost every case, the roadblocks I met were the result of *not following* the proven system to the letter, and skipping steps.

A word on skipping steps - *don't do it!* The same goes with not sticking with a program all the way through. From my own experiences, and from those I've heard in classes I've taught, it's become clear to me that when committing to a 'proven program,' skipping steps along the way - or giving up before you've put everything you had into it - will almost certainly lead to a dead end! This was another key motivating factor for me to write this book, and the workbook that goes with it; I want everyone to have a guide they can rely on for successful implementation of the ideas.

When it comes to team building, we must remember that while those trying their best deserve our time and attention, still - things don't always work out. Over the years, I've learned much from the hires that moved on - and (of course) even more from the people that remained with me. My job is to repay their commitment by removing any ceiling from their careers, and to create as much opportunity as possible *for each and every team member who really wants it.*

My key hires have come to form my 'leadership team,' and we meet weekly to discuss ideas, issues - and how to remain on track in order to meet our goals. Upon reflection, we've all agreed that these weekly meetings have been critical to our success - as so many perspectives are brought *to each point of discussion* - and with each leader engaged in arriving at positive outcomes. As a result of this, we are now the most successful sales team in Western North Carolina.

AllStarCertified Network

We're expanding the AllStarPowerhouse at Keller Williams brand around the country, through our expansion network. (See the current locations at www.AllStarPowerhouse.com.) The agents in the network are known as *AllStarCertified Agents,* who maintain their own branding and business while being supported by the programs and training through the network. We are on a talent search for one exclusive team (per Keller Williams Market Center) to join the AllStarCertified network. Each team will have access to all Programs featured in this book, one-on-one training (for their implementation), presentation materials, scripts and other benefits. Find out more at www.AllStarCertfied.com.

Here are the U.S. locations where we are carrying out our talent search.

I'm surrounded by truly amazing people - which includes all of the AllStarCertified agents - and remain acutely aware of how *the team is the success story.* AllStarPowerhouse @ Keller Williams success is borne from the KW platform, systems, models, and network of people who care for, and support each other through our training - which is second to none. AllStarCertified comprises local teams of truly unique individuals who share a common goal - and have the work ethic required to go with it.

Why do I do it? I've been told that those who come from difficult backgrounds can *learn from that experience,* and perhaps even convert it into 'achievement,' through grit and determination. Understandably, some will sit in a corner, shackled by the trauma.

As for me, I could never sit still for very long.

Acknowledgments

T hanks to everyone who has helped me in the amazing feat of publishing a book. I didn't think it would be easy, and - wow - what a ride. Love, Courage and Godspeed to:

My editor, Mark L. Hunt, for his patience, support and overview. This book benefits from his understanding the importance of constantly thinking of the reader, and without him it may well have died on the vine.

Contributing agents, and Real Estate Experts who offer their ideas and models throughout this book. Your input is invaluable.

Mike Kranz, my MAPS coach who keeps me sane and encouraged with his weekly dose of advice, support and insight. Murder, Divorce, Alzheimer's, Team restructuring - we've covered it all; you've guided me through my voyage of self-discovery, and occasionally *told me,* when I needed to be told!

My team, who must have wondered (after a year of talking about it) whether the book would really 'happen.' Special thanks to the leadership team, Jamie Jones, Patty Harron, Scott Angelo and Amber Reeves, you were there to grow the business, and lead the team, while my 'One Thing' was this book. You are my work family, and it's an honor to be in business with you.

Those agents and friends featured in the book who graciously shared their ideas and successes to help other agents succeed. Much gratitude for your mindset of 'abundance.'

Those who read the book as advance readers and gave valuable feedback, and contributions.

Tyler Elstrom, my friend and partner in the real estate expansion business.

Featured / Mentions:

Final Thoughts

I hope that you've enjoyed the thoughts, ideas, suggestions and Programs offered in this book. Most importantly, I hope you'll choose one which you feel passionately about, and *put it into action*, using the companion workbook and tools.

My goal was to provide action points, and if you can use any of the ideas herein to elevate your business to a higher level, then my purpose has been fulfilled.

The AllstarCertified.com network provides the license to use the programs covered in this book, presentation materials, forms and systems to support them, weekly training on how to use them and large discounts on CRM programs 'in a box' for one agent per market in a KW Market Center. Join the network for a flat fee with no commission sharing or loss of personal brand.

If you are interested in training on how to use the programs, a presentation at your location (or online), or joining the network, reach out to me @ www.UVPBook.com

"SHINE A LIGHT ON THE
PATH, SUCH THAT OTHERS
FIND THEIR MAGIC. WE'VE
ALL GOT IT. SOMETIMES IT'S
JUST HARD TO SEE."

ROWENA PATTON